LIVELY LESSONS

FOR
CLASSROOM SESSIONS
FOR GRADES 2–5

By
ROSANNE SHERITZ SARTORI

A great occasion to teach what's right
Is during counselors' sessions.
But kids don't listen long, it's true,
To these very important lessons.

Counselors fret that their words go unheard,
Kids ignoring much of what is said.
Research says they tune talk out,
Like word lists they have already read.

But if some spice is used to convey the point,
Like stories, songs, games, and raps,
The message will come through loud and clear,
And keep the kids from taking their naps!

DEDICATION

This book is dedicated to my husband, Glenn Sartori. Without his faith and love, I probably wouldn't have had the courage to submit my lessons for publication. He is a great listener and wonderful editor and he helped in numerous ways to get my manuscript ready for submission. I really could not have written this without his support.

I would also like to acknowledge my sister, Chris Flesor, who has been my personal cheerleader since childhood; my mother, Phyllis Sheritz, who was always generous with her praise and love; and my father, Milton Sheritz, who always encouraged me to strive for excellence and from whom I inherited my creative streak.

ROSANNE SHERITZ SARTORI

Rosanne Sheritz Sartori has been affiliated with the St. Charles School District in St. Charles, Missouri, as a teacher and counselor for more than 25 years. She has been a mentor for new teachers and counselors and a presenter of numerous inservice workshops for teachers, parenting classes, and state counselor workshops. St. Charles School District honored her with the Impact Award in 1985, 1988, and 1993; the Journey to Excellence Award in 1993, 1996, and 1997; and nominated her for Teacher of the Year in 1993.

Graphic images and borders © Eyewire images
Illustrations by Greg Griffith

Reprinted 2001
copyright © 2000 **mar*co products, inc.**

Published by **mar*co products, inc.**
1443 Old York Road
Warminster, PA 18974
1-800-448-2197

Library of Congress Catalog Card Number: 99-69980
ISBN: 1-57543-087-8
Printed in the U.S.A.

TABLE OF CONTENTS

INTRODUCTION

When I began preparing counseling lessons 12 years ago, I realized that my best lessons started with a story. It was a good way to begin the lesson and capture the attention of the students. With a story as a base, it was easy to teach what needed to be taught.

In the early years, I was always in the library or in book stores, looking for short books that would reinforce my lesson. I hardly ever found what I wanted. It was hard to find a book that was short enough to serve as an introduction and would still allow the facilitator enough time to teach the lesson. The books that I did find either didn't convey the right message or were too babyish for my audience. So I began to make up my own stories. These stories could include anything I needed them to include.

Along the way, I also realized that story-telling is a wonderful way to connect with students. If you have never experienced this connection, I urge you to try telling—not reading—the stories from this book. Eye contact is wonderful, and children use more imagination by listening and visualizing, rather than looking at pictures. If you tell the stories with enthusiasm and humor and use popular slang and terminology that students understand, the stories come alive.

Some of the stories in this book overlap. That's because I use different stories in different years or different stories in different grades. I have found that if I want to teach a lesson about organization, for example, I can basically use the same lesson for two years in a row if I change the stories. I have had fifth-graders tell me that they remember stories I told when they were in second grade. That's why it is important to keep track of which stories are told in which grades.

When you tell a story, try not to use the name of anybody in the classroom or, if possible, even in the school. You don't want a child to get teased because of something a character in a story does. Change the character's grade or age to match the audience's grade and age.

The lessons in this book are meant to entertain. Some educators may believe it unnecessary to entertain in order to get kids to listen. But if we want to make an impact, it's something we should *want* to do.

Kids sit all day in school and listen to their teachers. (If you have ever sat in a two-hour workshop, you know how hard this is!) So I think it is important that the counselor come in and do something different. When the kids go home and their parents ask what they learned in school, I want *my* lesson to be what they remember! That won't happen if I'm always giving the kids worksheets.

Puppets are great counseling tools, and you don't have to be a ventriloquist or smooth puppeteer to use them effectively. The kids have fun and don't judge your skills. If you are just too embarrassed to have your puppets talk out loud, have them whisper in your ear. Then tell the students what the puppet has said. The kids actually lean forward trying to hear what the puppet is saying.

Make this book usable for yourself. Mix and match the stories, activities, poems, and raps. The resulting lessons will be both meaningful and memorable.

Rosanne Sheritz Sartori

THE BIKE
A Lesson on Positive Attitude and Goal-Setting

MATERIALS NEEDED:

✔ Puppet
✔ Poster (page 10) reproduced and mounted
   on tag board or poster board
✔ Art paper, pencil, and crayons or markers for each student (optional)
✔ List of sayings that show perseverance, such as:
   "Rome wasn't built in a day."
✔ Copy of I "Can" (page 11) and pencil for each student
✔ Chalkboard and chalk

LESSON:

The facilitator should:

 Use a puppet to focus the students' attention. Introduce the puppet by name and have it act happy and excited. Then have the following conversation with the puppet:

> **Facilitator:** "Why are you so happy?"
> **Puppet:** "I'm happy because I got a good grade on a test."
> **Facilitator:** "That's great! Pride in yourself can be the best feeling in the world."

Ask the class:

"How many of you would like to do well in school and feel the same pride as (<u>NAME OF PUPPET</u>)? *(All of the students will raise their hands.)* I wonder how many of you really mean it and how many of you are just wishing it could be true. Well, today I'm going to tell you how you can make your wishes come true, and I'm going to begin by telling you a story."

 Read or tell the following story:

This is a story about two fourth-grade boys named Sam and Tony. *(In telling any story, try to choose names that nobody in the class has.)* **These boys have been best friends all of their lives. They live next door to each other, are the same age, and like many of the same things. They both like football, baseball, reading books, and eating chocolate ice cream. They haven't been in the same room at school each year, but that hasn't stopped them from being friends.**

One sunny Saturday, Sam and Tony were walking in their neighbor-hood. As they passed a bike shop, both boys stopped dead in their tracks. There, in the window, was the most beautiful bike anyone had ever laid eyes on! It was a neon orange mountain bike that looked like it could easily take any trail. Sam and Tony both said, "I WANT THAT BIKE!!!" The boys went into the shop and talked to the clerk about the bike. The clerk agreed with the boys when he said, "Yes, that bike cer-tainly is a beauty! The price is reasonable, too. It costs only $275." Sam and Tony looked at each other. The clerk might just as well have said $2,750, because neither of them had that kind of money.

But they *really* wanted that bike. So they did what most kids would do: They went home and asked their parents. "Mom, Dad, can I have $275?" they each asked. Guess what their parents said? *(The students love to answer this part: "NO!")*

You're right! Both boys heard the same answer, but they reacted in totally different ways. Sam said, "Oh, shucks! I guess I'll never have that bike." But Tony said, "Well, if my parents can't give me the money, I will find a way to earn it." Tony got busy. He started figuring out ways he could make money. He: *(Make up any way you can think of, having the students help.)*

- counted all the money in his piggy bank (about $3.17).
- asked neighbors for lawn and garden jobs.
- kept his eyes on the sidewalk, looking for lost change.
- gave up treats at school. (When his mom gave him money, he saved it!)
- started his own dog-walking business.
- searched the couch cushions in his house each night for loose change. (He asked his mom if he could do that.)
- went looking for reward posters for lost pets, then searched for the pets. (He found a couple, too!)
- saved tooth-fairy money.
- saved his birthday money.

To make a long story short, Tony did it! It took more than a year, but he saved that $275. And it was the proudest day in his life when he marched into that store and counted out dollars, dimes, and pennies. He got to ride the bike right out of the shop. Well, of course, the first person he wanted to show it to was his friend, Sam. Sam's eyes almost popped out of his head when he saw Tony ride up. "How did you do it?" Sam asked.

Tony's answer is so important that I wrote it down for you.

Display the poster with this statement:

"I believed I could do it, I didn't give up, and I made it come true."

 Discuss the story by asking the following questions:

"How did Tony get the bike?" *(He thought of ways he could make money and he saved the money he earned.)*

"Why didn't Sam get the bike?" *(When his parents wouldn't give him the money, he gave up.)*

Using the poster, analyze the statement Tony made by asking:

"What does **I believed I could do it** mean?" *(It shows that Tony had faith in himself. He had a positive "I can" attitude.)*

"What does **I didn't give up** mean?" *(It means that Tony was willing to do whatever it took to get the bike. It shows that he had perseverance.)*

"What does **I made it come true** show?" *(It shows that Tony set getting the bike as a realistic long-term goal, made a plan, and accomplished his long-term goal by setting short-term goals to make money.)*

Tell the students:

"If you want to succeed in school, you must make this same kind of commitment. You need to decide if you really want good grades as much as Tony wanted the bike or if you are just wishing for them like Sam wished for the bike, but not doing much to make your wish come true."

Decide whether to continue the lesson over three sessions, spending one whole lesson on each part of Tony's statement, or to cover the entire statement in one lesson.

Write **Positive Attitude** on the chalkboard. Then ask the students to name some important sports figures who have set records. Have the students describe what they think goes through an athlete's mind as he or she is playing a game. Explain that students need this same attitude in order to be successful in anything, including school. Give each student a piece of art paper, a pencil, and crayons or markers. Have the students design their own mottos or posters to remind themselves to be positive. (If you are using this as a separate lesson, do the *Jenny Can* story and lesson on pages 12-18.)

Write **Perseverance** on the chalkboard. Tell the students that *perseverance* means *not giving up* and that it goes hand in hand with a positive attitude. Discuss sayings such as: "Rome wasn't built in a day." and "If at first you don't succeed, try, try again." (If you are using this as a separate lesson, divide the students into groups and give each group a saying. Have each group explain its saying to the class.) Explain that Alexander Graham Bell made several hundred trials of his new idea (the telephone) before it actually worked. (If desired, include others who have had to persevere in order to succeed.) Use humor, such as: "If he had given up, we would be all be using carrier pigeons to deliver messages to each other."

Write **Goal-setting** on the chalkboard. Tell the students that all successful people set goals. However, even though it is important that their goals are realistic, they should not be afraid to make a stretch. Explain that goals should be measurable, that long-term goals should be broken down into short-term goals, and that planning is essential. Emphasize that big accomplishments don't just happen. (If you are using this as a separate lesson, do the *L-O-G* story and lesson on page 80.)

5 **Activity:** Distribute a copy of *I "Can"* and a pencil to each student. Have the students write some school goals and then plan what to do to accomplish them.

6 Conclude the lesson with this poem. Say the words that are in *italics* and tell the students they will say **Set a goal! Set a goal!** whenever you raise your hand. (If desired, you can reproduce the poem and assign different parts to groups of students.)

Set a goal! Set a goal!
If you want to achieve and succeed.
Set a goal! Set a goal!
You can accomplish any deed.
Set a goal! Set a goal!
Make it realistic, make it true.
Set a goal! Set a goal!
Be sure you'll be able to measure what you do.
Set a goal! Set a goal!
Stick with your plan 'till it's complete.
Set a goal! Set a goal!
Reward yourself when the goal you meet!
Set a goal! Set a goal!

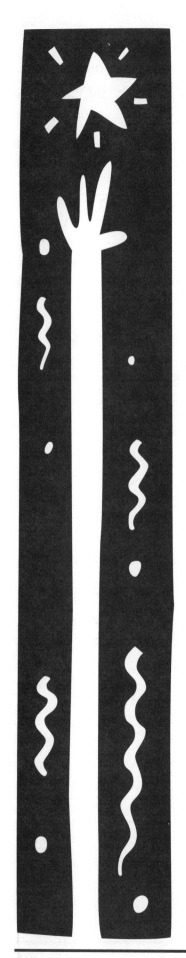

I believed I

could do it,

I didn't give up,

and I made

it come true.

I "CAN"

You can succeed in school if you plan and set goals for yourself. On the large can, write a long-term goal that you would like to accomplish. On the smaller cans, write the short-term goals that must be accomplished before you can successfully achieve the long-term goal.

JENNY CAN
A Lesson on the Importance of a Positive Attitude

MATERIALS NEEDED:

✔ Art paper, pencil, and crayons or markers for each student
✔ Magic wand (optional)

LESSON:

The facilitator should:

 Greet the class and tell the students that today's lesson is about a very important topic. In fact, it is the *most* important thing they will learn all year—more important than reading, writing, or arithmetic! *(This will get their attention and they will all want to know what you are talking about.)*

 Say to the students:

"Before I tell you what that subject is, I would like to tell you a story."

Read or tell the following story:

Jenny comes from a very large family. She is in fourth grade. Jenny is the youngest in a family of seven children! When you are the youngest child in a family that big, you are often called the "baby" of the family. Many times, you are treated like a baby even when you are in fourth grade.

Ask the students:

"How many of you are the 'baby' in your family?"

Continue reading or telling the story.

Anyway, being the baby can have its good points and its bad points. Jenny got lots of help, and sometimes it felt like she had six servants helping her. If she wanted a glass of milk, someone was always around to say, "Here, Jenny, I will pour it for you." If her room needed cleaning, she would cry and say, "I can't do it all by myself." One of her sisters or brothers would feel sorry for her and offer to help. There was always someone around who would sit with Jenny while she was doing her homework or help her with her chores.

That may sound great to you. But because Jenny got so much help, she started thinking that she *couldn't* do anything by herself. Most of the time, she didn't even *try* to do anything all by herself. In other words, she didn't have any confidence in herself and she developed a very poor attitude about herself.

When Jenny first started school, she was the kind of kid who was always up at the teacher's desk. "How do you do this?" she would ask. And since her teachers were kind, they would help her. But she would be up at the desk again and again. Jenny also took lots of her schoolwork home, because who do you think would be there to help her? *(Let the class answer: "Her brothers and sisters!")*

That is how it went until Jenny got to fourth grade. That year, her teacher was Mrs. Peterson. On the first day of school, Mrs. Peterson said, "Boys and girls, you are now in fourth grade. That means you are growing up, and I expect you to be very self-sufficient. Of course, I am here to teach you and give you support, but I expect you to use your own brains and think for yourselves.

Right then and there, Jenny began to get worried. She thought, "I can't do things by myself!"

Jenny's problems started right away. Mrs. Peterson gave the class some simple review problems to do in math. Jenny did what she usually did and went up to the teacher's desk right away. "How do you do these?" she asked.

Mrs. Peterson said, "Jenny, I am sure that if you sit down and try, you will be able to remember how to do these problems."

Jenny couldn't believe what she heard. "But I can't do them," she said.

Mrs. Peterson looked straight at Jenny and said, "Of course you can. Now sit down and remember what you learned last year."

Jenny knew then that she had the meanest teacher in the whole school. She sat at her desk and looked at the work. It was hopeless. She decided that she would take it home and get some help. And that is what she did.

This worked so well that Jenny decided that it was an excellent plan and she would do the same thing every day. She would pretend to do her work, then take everything home so that she could get help. And who do you think is going to help her? *(Let the class answer: "Her brothers and sisters!")*

Mrs. Peterson was pretty smart, and she began to notice that Jenny never got her work done at school. She also noticed that Jenny took all her books home and came to school with great-looking homework assignments.

One day, Mrs. Peterson decided to call Jenny's mom. She had only one question to ask: "Does Jenny get a lot of help at home?"

Jenny's mom thought that maybe Mrs. Peterson was hinting that Jenny needed more attention at home, and she answered, "I help her every night, and so do her father and all her brothers and sisters."

Mrs. Peterson said, "I think that is exactly Jenny's problem."

Jenny's mom was confused. She didn't understand what Mrs. Peterson meant. So Mrs. Peterson explained, "Somewhere along the line, Jenny got the idea that she *can't* do anything by herself. She needs to learn that she is capable and self-sufficient. I am going to ask all of you NOT to help Jenny in any way with her homework."

Jenny's mom felt terrible. She hadn't realized that all the help had *hurt* Jenny. She called all the older kids together and told them that they were not to help Jenny with her homework anymore.

That night, Jenny came home with lots of work. She started her math and said to one of her sisters, "I need help."

Her sister said, "I am sorry, Jenny. I can't help you."

Then Jenny went to one of her brothers and said, "I need help."

Her brother said, "I am sorry, Jenny, but I am not supposed to help you."

Jenny couldn't believe what she was hearing. How could they not help her? They *always* did. Jenny became so angry that she threw a temper tantrum! "I NEED HELP! I CAN'T DO THIS BY MYSELF! I NEED HELP! I WANT YOU TO HELP ME!"

Jenny's mom went to her and calmly said, "Jenny, I think we have helped you too much. You are a very smart young lady, and I think you can do this work by yourself."

Jenny started crying and sobbed, "I can't, I really can't."

Crying had always worked before, but this time Jenny's mom left her by herself. After she finished crying, Jenny sat at her desk and looked at her math problems. She felt so sorry for herself. "I am going to get an *F* on this assignment," she thought. "If they won't help me any-more, I am going to get an *F* on everything. I will have to repeat fourth grade, and I will be the oldest student ever to go to our school!"

With a frown on her forehead and a pout on her lips. Jenny sat at her desk looking at the first problem. She said, "I think I am supposed to subtract this first number, but you can't subtract 3 from 1. Oh, I don't know *what* I am doing. Maybe I will borrow from the next column."

Before long, Jenny had done the problem all by herself! She got so excited! It was the first problem she had ever done all by herself in her whole life. She thought, "Let me try the next one!" She did that one and the next one, and the one after that.

Jenny ended up doing the whole paper all by herself. She was so proud! She couldn't wait to see what grade she got. When her paper was graded and returned to her, Jenny saw that she had earned a *C*. And let me tell you, that *C* made her happier than a lot of the *A's* and *B's* she had made before. Why was this so? *(Let the class answer: "Because she did it all by herself.")*

That was the beginning of a lot of great things for Jenny. Now, if some-thing was really hard, she would remember the math paper she had done and she would think, "Well, I will try." And if one of her brothers or sisters started to help her with a big project, she would say, "Let me see if I can do it by myself."

Jenny grew up a lot that year, and her attitude really improved. She learned that she should trust herself, believe in herself, and always try hard.

One day, Jenny saw a little boy standing outside the kindergarten class-room door. He was crying. Jenny asked him what was wrong. The little boy said that he couldn't zip his jacket. Jenny started to do it for him. Then she thought of the problems that had been caused in her life be-cause everyone always helped her. She said to him, "I will show you how to do it, then I want you to try to do it by yourself. I know you can do it!"

And do you know what? HE DID IT!

 Discuss the story by asking the following question:

"At the beginning of the story, what was Jenny's problem?" *(Jenny did not be-lieve she could do anything by herself. She had a poor attitude about herself.)*

When someone mentions that Jenny had a poor attitude, say:

> "Yes, Jenny had a terrible attitude, and I think that having a good attitude is the most important thing you can do in order to be successful."

Remind the students that, at the beginning of the lesson, you said that this topic was the most important lesson they would learn all year. Emphasize that this is because none of us can succeed at anything if we don't believe in ourselves. Explain that people who believe in themselves have positive attitudes and that people who do not believe in themselves have negative attitudes. Then ask:

> "Who do you think does better in school?" *(Students with positive attitudes.)*

> "Who do you think does better in life?" *(People with positive attitudes.)*

Tell the students:

> "Many sports coaches give their teams a talk in the locker room before a big game. Do you think they say, 'You are all going to lose today!'? Does Mark McGwire or Sammy Sosa *(or any other well-known baseball player)* stand at the plate and say, 'I think I am going to strike out!'? NO! Positive attitude is an important part of any kind of success. In this story, Jenny didn't believe in herself. She really didn't try. She didn't even *know* what she could do."

Then ask:

> "Where did Jenny get her bad attitude?" *(Her family did everything for her. She never found out that she could do things for herself.)*

> "How do people get bad attitudes?" *(Bad attitudes come from failures, mistakes, the things we say to ourselves, ways that we compare ourselves to others, etc.)*

Tell the students:

> "Unfortunately, many students have bad attitudes. You can often tell what kind of attitude a person has from his or her body or face."

Select a student to come to the front of the room and demonstrate what a bad attitude looks like to other people. *(If needed, give the student help. Model poor posture and a face that is downcast.)* Reinforce the demonstration by saying, "Boy, that sure looks like a poor attitude!" Then ask a student to show what a person with a good attitude would look like. *(If needed, give the student help. Model good posture and a confident or smiling face.)*

Say to the students:

> "Research has shown that people who smile more are more successful at what they do. Why do you think this is so?" *(Accept any appropriate answers.)*

Tell the students:

"Although the image you portray on the *outside* is important, what is going on *inside* is even *more* important. We all talk to ourselves every day. We say things like, 'I can really do good work.' or 'I am so stupid, I can't do anything right!' Which is the good attitude?" *(I can really do good work is the good attitude.)*

"Some students have a negative attitude because they say they can't, just like Jenny did in the story. Some students with a negative attitude say, 'I won't!' For example, the teacher might ask everyone to work quietly. We all know people who don't want to do that!"

Tell the class that you can prove that having a good attitude is important and will make a person more successful. Then proceed with the following activity.

 Activity: Ask pairs of students to come to the front of the room and demonstrate the difference that having a good attitude can make. Have one student role-play what someone with a negative attitude would think, say, and do in the following situations. Have the other student role-play what someone with a positive attitude would think, say, and do.

- **Talking on stage in front of the whole school.** *(If the students need help, coach them and give them hints.)* Explain that the person with a negative attitude would say: "I can't do this, I am so nervous, I am going to be sick." Then have the student show what a person thinking such thoughts would look like on the stage. The performance definitely wouldn't be one of confidence. Then explain what the person with the positive attitude would say: "I am enjoying being in front of everyone. I know I can do a good job." Then have the students show what that person would look like on the stage.

- **Learning to ice skate.** Give the students the same coaching as before, having the person with the negative attitude fear falling down and the person with the positive attitude show that he/she has good balance and can ice skate.

- **Batting in a baseball game.** Continue with the same coaching, having the person with the negative attitude be certain of striking out and the person with the positive attitude determined to hit the ball out of the park.

Ask the students to sit down. Continue the lesson by saying that the key to school success is for them to show a positive attitude before they begin any task that will be asked of them in (<u>NAME THE GRADE THEY ARE IN</u>).

Then say:

"Now I know that not everyone has such a positive attitude. But luckily, I know a little magic. *(Use a magic wand or just wiggle your fingers.)* Who would like to come to the front of the room?" *(Select a student.)*

Have the student face the class. Then say:

> "I'm sure you are not one of those people with a negative attitude, but just pretend that you are. Show us what your negative attitude would look and sound like in this situation. I will pretend that I am your teacher and I will say, 'Today, we are going to learn how to do a new type of math problem.' " *(After all of the previous demonstrations, the students will probably know they should look upset and say: "I am no good at math.")*

Then say:

> "That is a bad attitude! Now for the magic! I will change this negative attitude into a good attitude. Presto! Chango!" *(Wave the wand or wiggle your fingers. Most students will get the joke, look eager, and say: "I can do this!")*

Repeat the activity several more times, always pretending to be the teacher. Each time, let a student pretend to have a bad attitude, then *magically* change it into a *good* attitude. Use such examples as:

- Today we are going to write a story.
- I need you to work quietly at your desk.

By this time, many students will be volunteering to be the student whose attitude is *magically* changed.

Then say:

> "Let's all try it together. Pretend that I am the teacher and my whole class is showing me a negative attitude when I say, 'This year, you will be learning many new things, and some of them will be difficult.' " *(The class will groan loudly and say things like: "I can't do it!")*

Then say:

> "Presto! Chango!" *(All the students will sit up and look eager.)*

When this happens, say:

> "This is the way I want to see you look all year."

If the classroom teacher is in the room, tell him/her to remember to use the *Presto! Chango!* magic during the school year, whenever a bad attitude is noticed. When someone is struggling with a difficult task, this activity often lightens the mood considerably.

 Activity: Conclude the lesson by distributing a piece of art paper, a pencil, and crayons or markers to each student. Have the students design a *Can Do* poster that can be displayed in the classroom, kept in their desks, or hung in their rooms at home.

CINDY AND SANDY
A Lesson on Responsibility

MATERIALS NEEDED:

✔ Puppet
✔ Copy of *Responsibility Guidelines* (page 23) and pencil for each student group
✔ Copy of *Am I Responsible?* (page 24) and pencil for each student
✔ Copy of *I'm Responsible, I Take Care of Me* (page 25); and yellow, blue, and red crayons for each student (optional)

LESSON:

The facilitator should:

 Use a puppet to focus the students' attention. Then have the following conversation with the puppet:

Facilitator: "What did you do over the weekend?"
Puppet: "After my homework and chores were done, I went to the park."
Facilitator: "Do you have many chores to do?"
Puppet: *(matter-of-factly)*, "Well, on Saturdays, I always clean my own room and do my part with family chores, like taking out the trash and dusting the furniture."
Facilitator: "You do those chores every weekend?"
Puppet: "Yes, those chores are my Saturday jobs. During the week, my job is to keep up with my schoolwork, set the table for dinner, and help with the dishes."
Facilitator: "It sounds like you really do your part. I can think of a great word to describe you." *(Either tell the students, have them guess what word you are thinking of, or play* Wheel of Fortune *on the chalkboard to introduce the term* responsible.*)*

Discuss the meaning of *responsibility* by having the students describe the actions that are taken by a responsible person. These actions should include:

• taking care of yourself and your belongings.
• being dependable and doing jobs that you are expected to do.
• making good decisions.
• being able to admit when you are wrong and to remedy your mistakes.
• helping out even without being asked.

Mar✶co Products, Inc.

Read or tell the following story, adding—or letting the students add—details. Present the story playfully and dramatically.

Cindy and Sandy are identical twins. If you ever met them, you would have a hard time telling who is Cindy and who is Sandy because they look exactly alike and they love to dress alike.

But even though Cindy and Sandy look just alike, they have very different personalities:

- **Cindy likes dolls.**
- **Sandy likes sports.**
- **Cindy likes healthy food (like oranges and apples).**
- **Sandy likes sweets (like cookies and candy).**
- **Cindy is good at math.**
- **Sandy is good at reading.**

And there is another way that they are really different:

- **Cindy is responsible.**
- **Sandy isn't !**

At home, Cindy shows that she is responsible by _____ .

(Let the students help you fill in this part of the story. Their answers should include: cleaning up after herself, admitting mistakes, keeping herself clean, doing chores, etc.)

At school, Cindy shows she is responsible by _____ .

(Let the students again help you fill in the details. Answers should include: doing her work, following rules, keeping her desk organized, etc.)

At home, Sandy _____ .

(Let students say what Sandy does. Students really enjoy describing what a slob she is!)

And at school, Sandy _____ .

(Let the students answer.)

Because the girls are so different, they are treated differently. Once, a neighbor asked their mom if one of the girls could water his plants while he was on vacation. He said that he would be happy to pay her for taking care of his plants. The twins' mom said, "Cindy can do it."

At the twin's house, there is a rule: TV isn't turned on until homework is finished. Well, Cindy *always* gets to watch her favorite show, but Sandy *never* gets to see hers!

A Saturday rule is that when chores are finished, the girls can go out to play. Cindy gets to play, but Sandy doesn't! And on Saturday, if chores have been done, the girls get their allowance. Cindy always gets paid, but Sandy never gets her money!

Sandy started to notice the better treatment Cindy got, and she went to their mom to complain. She whined, "Mom, you love Cindy more than me."

Her mom asked, "Sandy, why would you say that?"

Sandy said, "Because you treat her better!"

Mom said, "Sandy, your father and I love both of you girls equally. It's just that Cindy can be counted on because she has learned to be more responsible than you are. And privileges usually come with responsibility."

"How do you become responsible?" asked Sandy.

Her mom explained that once a person decides responsibility is important, he or she works hard to act that way. "It's not always easy," she told Sandy, "but if Cindy can do it, I'll bet you can, too!"

Sandy decided right then that she wanted to be responsible, and she began thinking of ways to improve.

And you know what? Now when a neighbor asks their mom for a helper, she says, *(practice and say these next lines quickly)* "Sandy or Cindy can do it." AND Sandy and Cindy watch TV together, AND Sandy and Cindy play on Saturday, AND Sandy and Cindy get paid their allowance BECAUSE...

SANDY AND CINDY ARE RESPONSIBLE !

 Discuss the story by asking the following questions:

"How did Cindy show that she was responsible?" *(She did what was expected of her.)*

"What does a responsible person do?" *(A responsible person does the jobs that are expected (at school and at home) with good effort and with little or no reminding, takes care of him/herself and takes care of his/her belongings, thinks through decisions, admits to a mistake and tries to remedy the situation, helps out even when not asked, etc.)*

Divide the students into small groups. Give each group a *Responsibility Guidelines* worksheet and a pencil. Tell the students:

> "It is your turn to make up stories, and each group is to make up two stories. The stories should be about a very responsible child or about a child who is not responsible. You may make up one story about a responsible child and one story about a child who is not responsible or you may make up two stories of the same kind. Choose one person from your group to be responsible for writing your stories down and one to be responsible for reading the stories to the class. When your stories are read to the class, your classmates will have to decide if you are writing about a responsible person or about a person who is not responsible."

When all the stories have been read, distribute a copy of *Am I Responsible?* and a pencil to each student. Then say:

> "It is now time to admit if you act like the people in the responsible stories you have heard or if you act like the people in the irresponsible stories. You can do this by completing the *Am I Responsible?* activity sheet. You will not be asked to share your answers with the class, but it is important that you answer honestly. The activity sheet will not to be collected or graded. It is only for you to think about."

Optional Activity: Distribute a copy of *I'm Responsible, I Take Care of Me!* and a yellow, red, and blue crayon to each student. Have the students follow the directions at the bottom of the activity sheet. Allow them to take the completed activity sheet home.

Conclude the lesson with the following rap. Say the words that are in *italics* and tell the students they will say **Responsible, responsible** whenever you raise your hand.

Responsible, responsible
Do your work each day.
Responsible, responsible
All jobs done before you play.
Responsible, responsible
People count on you.
Responsible, responsible
You'll be proud and happy, too.
Responsible, responsible
A wonderful way to be,
Responsible, responsible
Then you can say, "I take care of me!"

RESPONSIBILITY GUIDELINES

A responsible person:

1. does all of his/her jobs at school and at home with good effort and with little or no reminding.
2. takes care of himself/herself and his/her belongings.
3. makes well-thought-out decisions.
4. can admit to making a mistake and try to remedy the situation.
5. will help out even when he/she is not asked to do so.

STORY #1

_____

_____

_____

_____

_____

STORY #2

_____

_____

_____

_____

 # AM I RESPONSIBLE?

Rate yourself on the following statements by circling the correct answer.
BE HONEST!

1.	I keep up with all my assignments.	Always	Sometimes	Hardly ever
2.	I follow class and school rules.	Always	Sometimes	Hardly ever
3.	I do my chores at home.	Always	Sometimes	Hardly ever
4.	I do chores without being told.	Always	Sometimes	Hardly ever
5.	I help even when I am not asked to.	Always	Sometimes	Hardly ever
6.	I take care of my belongings.	Always	Sometimes	Hardly ever
7.	I think through decisions.	Always	Sometimes	Hardly ever
8.	I can admit my mistakes.	Always	Sometimes	Hardly ever
9.	My parents trust me.	Always	Sometimes	Hardly ever
10.	I take care of my grooming.	Always	Sometimes	Hardly ever
11.	I take care of my health.	Always	Sometimes	Hardly ever
12.	I try to be on time.	Always	Sometimes	Hardly ever
13.	People can count on me.	Always	Sometimes	Hardly ever

Complete the following statements:

1 I am responsible in the following ways:

_____

_____

_____

2 I need to improve in the following ways:

_____

_____

_____

3 My goal for this week is:

_____

_____

_____

I'M RESPONSIBLE, I TAKE CARE OF ME

**Use the yellow crayon to color the areas with dots.
Color the other areas red or blue.**

THE PERFECT LESSON
A Lesson on Self–Acceptance

MATERIALS NEEDED:

- ✔ Puppet
- ✔ 2 magazine pictures or drawings of a child (one of a boy, the other of a girl) engaged in an activity like skating or playing ball
- ✔ Copy of *Nobody's Perfect…Not Even Me!* (page 33) and a pencil for each student (optional)

LESSON:

The facilitator should:

 Use a puppet and make it look very sad. Give the puppet a name, and introduce it to the class. Then have the following conversation with the puppet:

Facilitator: "Why are you sad?"
Puppet: "I didn't do well on my math test."
Facilitator: "Oh, that's too bad. What grade did you get?"
Puppet: *(looking even sadder and whispering)* "I got a 92."
Facilitator: *(Look at the class with a puzzled expression on your face.)* "How many of you would be sad to get a 92 on a test? There are people who are very hard on themselves and who never seem to be satisfied with anything they do."

2 Tell the class that you want to tell them a story about a boy who is just like (<u>NAME OF THE PUPPET</u>). Then read or tell the following story:

Steve Sanders is a 10–year–old boy who lives with his mom and older sister in a small house in a suburb of a large city. Steve is a nice boy who smiles frequently and is quite friendly. If you ever met him, you would probably like him. Besides being nice, Steve is funny and smart and, to top it off, is very good in sports. Most of Steve's friends think very highly of him. There is one person, though, who is very critical of Steve, and that is Steve himself! You see, he is very hard on himself. He expects a lot and gets very frustrated when he doesn't live up to his own expectations.

At school, for example, Steve always wants and expects to get 100% whenever his class has a spelling test. It is wonderful when a person tries hard and puts forth a lot of effort, but Steve takes it one step further. He won't accept anything less than 100%! One week, Steve missed one word on his spelling test. Inside his head, he was angry with himself and said, "You are so stupid! You knew how to spell that word! Why can't you ever do anything right?" In fact, the missed spelling word upset him for the rest of the day.

Math is a very difficult subject for Steve, so he often yells at himself about his math grades. One week, his class took a big math test on fractions and Steve missed five problems. Some of his classmates who missed just as many were relieved and satisfied. But not Steve. "I can't believe how careless and ignorant I am," he said to himself on the way home.

Steve is like this not only at school. He is like this about everything. He is on a baseball team called the Bobcats. One time, in the ninth inning of an important championship game, Steve hit a grand slam home run and helped his team win the game. You'd think Steve would be happy about that. But after the game, all he could think about was that in the second inning, he had fumbled the ball when trying to throw it to first base. "What is wrong with me? Why do I always have to be so clumsy?" he grumbled.

Even on his birthday, Steve didn't give himself a break. He missed two questions on a science quiz and missed four problems on a math paper. He was mad at himself all the way home.

When he got home, his mom greeted him with a big smile and a cheery, "Happy Birthday!" She asked him how his day had gone, and Steve said, "Awful! As usual, I was the dumbest kid in class!"

Steve's mom said, "Oh, Steve, I hate to hear you talk that way! You are NOT dumb!" She continued, "Let's just forget about school. I made your favorite dinner, spaghetti and meatballs, and I baked a chocolate birthday cake. And I got some very special birthday candles to put on top of your cake!"

Steve asked, "What could be special about candles?"

"Well," his mom said, "it was funny. I was leaving for the store to buy candles, and this little man was outside on the sidewalk with a pushcart. He was selling lots of stuff. When I asked him if he had any candles, he said that he had some magic candles. The man told me that when you blow them out, your wishes will come true!"

"Do you believe him? Do you think that it's for real?" Steve asked excitedly.

"Well, Steve," his mom answered, with a smile on her face and a twinkle in her eye, "I don't know if I believe in magic, but I guess you'd better be careful about what you wish for!"

Steve couldn't wait for his birthday dinner! That evening, the whole family enjoyed the spaghetti and meatballs. Then his mom brought out the cake. The candles *did* look weird. They were brown, and fatter than most standard birthday candles. When it was time, Steve's mom lit the candles and she and his sister joined together to sing *Happy Birthday to You*. When they finished singing, Steve shut his eyes and wished, "I wish I was perfect!" Then he took a deep breath and blew out the candles.

Steve was so excited! He couldn't wait to see if his wish had come true. For the first few days, he just couldn't tell. He got 100% on several papers and on the spelling test, but Steve's grades were usually pretty good anyway. But when he got 100% on a six-page test covering everything the class had learned in math all year, Steve knew his wish had come true!

"YES!!!" he shouted. Everyone in his class turned to look at him. Steve blushed and said, "Excuse me."

Being perfect was fantastic! Steve got 100% on every paper he turned in. He NEVER made a mistake in school. And in baseball, he was a star! He hit a homer every time he got up to bat, and he never made any errors when he was fielding. Steve really enjoyed himself...for a while.

Then something funny happened. Steve began to get bored! He didn't even look at the *A's* on his papers after a while. The excitement was gone. It was all so predictable.

His mother also began taking all those perfect papers for granted. After a while, Steve would come home and say in a bored tone, "Mom, I got 100% on the Stanford Achievement Test." His mom would reply in an equally bored tone, "That's nice, dear."

The excitement was gone in baseball, too. Steve always knew he would hit a home run when he was at bat, so there wasn't any thrill to it. Even the spectators were bored when Steve was at bat! "Oh, it's that kid who always hits home runs," some of them said. "Let's go get a soda while he's batting."

By the time Steve's birthday rolled around again, he was sure he had made the wrong wish. He went to his mom and asked, "Mom, have you seen that funny little man with the pushcart lately?"

At first, Steve's mom looked blank. When she remembered who he was talking about, she answered, "No, honey. I never saw him again after that one day."

"Do we have any of those weird candles left?" Steve asked hopefully.

"I think I saw one the other day in the junk drawer," his mom replied.

Steve ran to the junk drawer. He pulled out string and tape and tooth-picks and bread ties and lots of other junk. And there, in the bottom of the drawer, was one bent brown candle!

"Mom, are you going to make me a birthday cake this year?" he asked.

"You know I always do, Steve. Why do you ask?"

"Well, could we use this candle on top?" he asked, showing her the brown candle.

"But Steve, it's all bent and broken," his mom protested.

"Please, Mom." begged Steve. "It's really important!"

So Steve's mom placed the one brown candle on the top of his birth-day cake. After his sister and his mom sang *Happy Birthday*, Steve looked at the cake and hoped that one candle would do the job. Then he closed his eyes and wished, "I wish I was just regular Steve again."

At first, Steve really couldn't tell whether his wish had come true. In the next few days, he got several papers back with 100% on them, but Steve's grades had always been pretty good anyway. But when he got back his big math paper with four problems marked wrong, he knew his wish had come true.

"YES!!" Steve shouted. Everyone looked at him, especially his teacher. She was surprised at his excitement over his grade when he usually had a perfect paper. Steve blushed and said, "Excuse me."

Steve ran home that day and yelled to his mom, with great excite-ment in his voice, "Mom, I missed four problems on my math test!"

His mom looked at him with a puzzled expression on her face and said, "Well, that's nice, dear!"

Steve's mom didn't understand his excitement, but he had learned a very important lesson. He was going to have to try hard and strive to achieve again. Sometimes he was going to have the thrill of experiencing perfection, but sometimes he was going to experience the anguish of making mistakes and the frustration of occasional failures. But Steve now knew that it is not the perfection of every act that matters. It is the joy of striving and trying and reaching for the top that makes everything worthwhile!

3 Discuss the story by asking the following questions:

"How do you feel when you have taken a test and the teacher is passing back the papers?" *(Excited, worried, hopeful, etc.)*

"If you knew what grade would be on the paper, would you still have these feelings?" *(No, because you would already know what grade you were getting.)*

 Tell the students:

"We all have strengths and weaknesses. We all have things at which we excel or do well and those we struggle with. Students who struggle with many school subjects could start to think that they can't do anything well. They could begin to feel bad about themselves and then stop even trying. This should not happen. Being perfect should not be your goal because, as you have heard before, NO ONE is perfect! Your only goal should be to strive to do the very best you can. If this is better than someone else or worse than someone else, it does not matter. The only thing that matters is that you are striving to do your best."

"By knowing and admitting our strengths and weaknesses, we are helping ourselves. We can feel proud of strengths. We can gain by admitting that we have to work hard on our weaknesses. And no matter how smart we are or what age we are, we all have weaknesses."

5 Show one magazine picture or drawing. Tell the students:

"The (BOY/GIRL) in this picture loves (NAME OF ACTION THE CHILD IS PERFORMING). To be honest, (HE/SHE) is not very good at it, but (HE/SHE) has a lot of fun doing it, and that is what is important. (HIS/HER) big dream is to (NAME SOME GOAL LIKE: PLAY IN A SUPER BOWL OR COMPETE IN THE OLYMPICS. NAME A GOAL RELATIVE TO THE ACTION DESCRIBED ABOVE) some day. (HE/SHE) may or may not do it, but (HE/SHE) sure tries and practices and dreams and has a great time."

Show the students the second picture and discuss it in a similar manner.

 Activity: Present the following activity. It can help a class become cohesive and help some students stop feeling defensive and embarrassed about their weaknesses. In the activity, students admit that they need to work hard to succeed in certain areas. Sit on a chair in the front of the room. Tell the students:

"We are going to play a game called *I Am Special.* In this game, we are going to admit to others that we have strengths we can be proud of, but that we also have weaknesses. Should we be embarrassed, ashamed, and give up because we have weaknesses? NO! It just means that we have to work harder in those areas. I will start by reciting a little rhyme. If you are good at the things I am good at, stand up."

"I try hard,
And so do you.
Whoever is good at _____, *(Name something you do well.)*
Stand up, too!"

"Everyone who feels he or she has this strength should be standing up with me. Some of us are standing and some are sitting. Does that mean that those of us standing are more special? No, it just means that (TRAIT OR TALENT NAMED) is just our thing! Let's find out what other people's strengths are."

Continue the activity by having students recite the rhyme, telling the class a strength each of them has, and having the other members of the class stand if they have the same strength. Encourage the students to think of all kinds of things, not just school subjects. *(For example, taking care of little brothers and sisters, mowing the lawn, etc.)*

If you see someone who doesn't stand for anything, say that some students seem to be too hard on themselves, like Steve. Explain that you don't have to be *perfect* at the things mentioned in order to be *good* at them. To avoid having any student left out of the activity, have every student take a turn saying one thing that he/she is good at.

After playing for a while, stop and say:

"We have enjoyed naming things we do well, but now we have to admit that we all have weaknesses, too. We are going to change the rhyme and talk about things we struggle with. You are not allowed to say you are bad at something, only that it is something you have to work hard at. I am going to start. If you need to work hard at the thing I mention, stand up."

"I try hard,
And so do you,
Whoever has to work hard at _____, *(Name something you have to work*
Stand up, too!" *hard at. Be truthful with the kids.)*

Continue the game as before, having the students name things they need to work at. At first, the students may look around to see who is standing when they stand, but they gain confidence as the game progresses.

 Optional Activity: Distribute a copy of *Nobody's Perfect...Not Even Me!* and a pencil to each student. Have the students complete the activity sheet. They may share their answers with the class if they so desire.

Conclude the lesson by telling the students:

> "Winning every time or getting 100% on every assignment should not be your objective. To strive and practice and keep trying is what is important and what counts."

Take the puppet out and ask if it feels better about the 92% on the math test. Make the puppet look happy and say:

> "I tried hard and it worked!"

NOBODY'S PERFECT...NOT EVEN ME!
(But I am proud of myself anyway!)

Full name _____

Birthday _____ Place of birth _____

Some things I enjoy doing:

1. _____
2. _____
3. _____
4. _____
5. _____

I am good at:

1. _____
2. _____
3. _____
4. _____
5. _____

I have to work hard at:

1. _____
2. _____
3. _____
4. _____
5. _____

I am proud of myself because _____

_____

_____

_____ .

THE KING'S GARDEN
A Lesson on Self–Esteem

MATERIALS NEEDED:

- ✔ Silk flowers (one branch of violets, one pink rose, one yellow daffodil, and a tulip) to make the story more dramatic during the telling (optional)
- ✔ Chalkboard and chalk or chart paper and marker with poem (page 36) written on it
- ✔ Copy of *I Am Unique* (page 37) and a pencil for each student (optional)

LESSON:

The facilitator should:

 Introduce the lesson by greeting the students and telling them that today's lesson will be about something very important.

 Tell the class that you are going to begin with a story. Then read or tell the following story:

> Once upon a time, there was a king who loved flowers. He thought that nothing was as beautiful as a field of flowers...not a rainbow, nor the blue ocean, nor a majestic forest. He wished all the people in his kingdom felt the same way, because he thought it would be wonderful to have his entire kingdom covered with blooming flowers.
>
> One night, as he lay in bed, the king tried to come up with a plan that would encourage people to plant gardens full of beautiful flowers. All of a sudden, a simple idea came to him. He would hold a contest!
>
> The next day, the king sent men on horses to travel throughout the kingdom and announce the contest. The person who could grow the most beautiful garden would win a treasure chest full of gold and jewels. When the people heard the king's plan, they became very excited. Everyone began to plant a garden, hoping to win the contest.
>
> The king's coachman planted a garden full of tulips that were gorgeous. He knew that the king liked tulips, because he always said so on their drives through the kingdom. *(Hold up the silk tulip.)* When the king saw it he said, "I love tulips, and this is a very beautiful garden. But I'm sorry, I don't think that it is the *most beautiful* garden in the kingdom."
>
> Meanwhile, the king's baker said, "Well, I know what the king likes. Whenever he orders a cake, he always requests that roses made of

icing be put on the top. I know he loves roses, especially pink ones. That's what I will grow in my garden."

So the baker planted some wonderful pink roses. *(Hold up the silk rose.)* The king raved about that garden when he saw it. He said, "The color of these roses is breathtaking, and I do love roses, but I am afraid that I wouldn't consider this the most beautiful garden."

The contest went on and on. Many people thought that they knew just what kind of flower the king would probably like and they planted gardens full of beautiful blooms. Each time the king saw another garden, he would smile and compliment his subject, then announce that this was not the winning garden.

One day a (<u>GRADE LEVEL TO WHICH THE STORY IS BEING PRESENTED</u>) grade teacher had just given an assignment and was watching her class work. As she watched the children, her thoughts began to wander. She thought of the king's contest and how much the treasure would mean to these children. If she could only think of some way to win the contest! But she knew nothing about flowers, only children. She watched their beautiful faces and thought about how different each child was. Suddenly she was struck with an idea! She couldn't wait until she could go home and begin planting.

The teacher planted and watered and cared lovingly for her garden. Finally, it was ready for the king to come and see it. When he arrived, he was awestruck. It certainly WAS the most beautiful garden he had ever seen. Can anyone guess what the garden looked like? The teacher had planted one of every kind of flower. *(Hold up bouquet of all flowers.)* Just like the children, no two were the same.

The king announced that the teacher had won the contest. He ordered that she be awarded the chest full of gold and jewels. She took it right to school to share with her class. She knew that she couldn't keep the treasure for herself. The children of her class had earned it. They had been her inspiration.

 Discuss the story by asking the following questions:

"Why was the teacher's garden the most beautiful?" *(The fact that the garden was full of different kinds of flowers made it beautiful.)*

"What was it about the class that gave the teacher the idea for planting such a garden?" *(When she looked at her class and saw how the children's differences made them beautiful, she thought that the garden would also be beautiful if it was filled with different kinds of flowers.)*

"What are some ways that we are all alike?" *(We all have feelings, have families, want to be liked, etc.)*

"What are some ways that we are different?" *(Encourage the students to be open about differences in skin color, religion, rates of learning, strengths, weaknesses, etc.)*

Tell the students that our differences actually make us who we are and that we all need to learn to appreciate the differences instead of comparing ourselves *(sometimes negatively)* to others.

Ask the students:

"What does the word *unique* mean?" *(It means being different from everything else. Nobody in the world is quite the same as anybody else, and that* unique-ness *makes everyone very special. Even twins are unique. No matter how much twins may look alike, they are still different people. One may like math and the other like reading, or one may like broccoli and the other, cauliflower. Twins are as unique as anyone else.)*

Activity: Distribute a copy of *I Am Unique* and a pencil to each student. Ask the students to complete the activity sheet. Encourage them to be proud of who they are.

When the students have completed the activity sheet, ask them to look at the line on which they wrote their names. Tell them that their names were chosen specially for them. Then ask any of the children who knows how his/her name was chosen to share his/her story with the class. Have those who know tell whom they were named after. *(Many children don't appreciate first or middle names. Try to get them to realize the uniqueness of names.)*

Collect the activity sheets. Tell the students that you are going to play a guessing game. Read some of the information from the sheets without mentioning the authors' names. Have the students guess who is being described. *(Students like to hear information read out loud.)* Read as much information as it takes to have the students identify the author. Tell the students that they are so unique that people can identify them by just sharing a few facts.

Conclude the lesson with the poem below. Point to the chart paper or chalkboard. Divide the group into two parts. Have one group say the words in *italics,* and have the other group say the words in **bold** type.

There's no one in the world like me!
I'm unique, I said unique!
Being one of a kind is great, you see.
I'm unique, I said unique!
My hair, my eyes, my face, are mine.
I'm unique, I said unique!
I'm proud that I'm a one-of-a-kind design.
I'm unique, I said unique!

I AM UNIQUE

My birthday is _____ .

The earliest birthday I can remember is _____ .

Something I have done that I'm proud of is _____

_____ .

What I would like to do this weekend is _____

_____ .

Some strengths I have are _____

_____ .

Some things I am working to get better at are ___

_____ .

The best thing about my family is _____

_____ .

My full name is _____ .

Color of my eyes: _____

Color of my hair: _____

My favorite food: _____

My favorite sport: _____

My favorite song: _____

My favorite color: _____

My favorite subject: _____

My favorite time of day: _____

THE SECRET WEAPON
A Lesson on Kindness

MATERIALS NEEDED:

✔ A decorated shoe box—with a slit in the lid—labeled *Friendship Box*
✔ Copy of *Friendship Worksheet* (page 43) and a pencil for each student

LESSON:

The facilitator should:

 Tell the students that you are going to tell them a story about a class whose students were so mean that their teacher didn't even want to come to school each day. Then read or tell the following story:

Last year, Mrs. Timmons' (<u>GRADE LEVEL TO WHICH THE STORY IS BEING PRESENTED</u>) grade class was known as the meanest class at Francis School.

If you went to that school, you would know that it had nothing to do with Mrs. Timmons. In fact, she was really nice, and a good teacher. But last year, some of the rudest and meanest students who ever attended Francis School were assigned to her class. They were rude with a capital *R*! They just didn't seem to like each other at all. From the first day of school, everyone treated everyone else horribly. They insulted each other, made fun of each other, butted in front of each other in lines, and were selfish. Mrs. Timmons' class was just not a nice place to be.

It would start every morning. The students came into class noisily and, of course, each one wanted to be first. Everyone would push and shove others away from the door. And right away the insults would start. "Get out of my way, stupid!" was a common greeting.

One morning, Susie came to school with a new haircut. You should have heard the comments her classmates made as she walked into the room! Even though her hair looked really good, she heard comments like, "You look like you got your head caught in a lawn mower."

When gym time came, it was even worse. Talk about poor sports! They cheated and complained, bragged if they won, and got mad if they lost. Nobody had any fun.

Let me tell you one example of how selfish they were. On Darryl's birthday, his mom baked cupcakes for the class. The problem was, Darryl didn't want to share them with anyone. He ate six of them himself and threw the rest away.

Poor Mrs. Timmons! She had to face this class every day. Sometimes she didn't even feel like coming to school.

One day, Mrs. Timmons was in the teachers lounge, telling a few other teachers how mean her students were to each other. The teachers started giving her suggestions about how she could get her students to be nice to each other.

"How about if you reward them when you see something good happen?" suggested one of the teachers.

"Good idea," thought Mrs. Timmons. "I'll try that." So she bought some candy and decided she would give a piece to any student she saw being nice to someone. She thought that maybe the other kids would want to try to earn candy, too, and they would *all* start being nice. Do you know what, though? She wasn't able to give even one piece of candy away! So that idea didn't work at all.

Mrs. Timmons was in the teachers lounge one day, looking very forlorn. Another teacher asked her what was wrong. Mrs. Timmons told the teacher how unkind her students were. The teacher suggested that Mrs. Timmons punish the students when she saw someone being unkind. The teacher said, "Why don't you take away one minute of recess when someone acts mean?"

"Good idea," thought Mrs. Timmons. "I'll try that." The first day she tried it, her class had no recess. The second day, they had no recess. And the third day, they had no recess. By this time, they were getting even more foul-tempered because they were feeling cooped-up, restless, and edgy. Mrs. Timmons soon gave up this plan.

After these two experiences, Mrs. Timmons gave up. She came to school every day and tried to referee the students.

One day, a new kid named Kevin was assigned to the class. How would you like to be a new kid in that class? *(Stop the story and allow the students to answer.)*

The kids didn't smile, didn't offer to show Kevin around, and certainly didn't make him feel welcome! But it didn't seem to matter to Kevin. He came in that first day and smiled. Then he said, "I'm really glad to meet all of you! I think I am going to like it here." Everyone looked at Kevin like he had just landed from Mars.

They had never known anyone like Kevin! He certainly had the best manners of anyone they had ever met. He always said, "Please," and "Thank you," and "Why don't you go first?"

He brought some cookies to school on his second day and said, "My mom bakes great cookies, and I wanted to share these with my new friends." He smiled at each kid as he handed each of them a cookie.

In gym, Kevin was a great sport. He always complimented people on their skills and said, "Good game!" at the end, whether his team won or lost.

Kevin became very popular. People seemed to feel good when they were with him. He had this talent for making everyone feel special. So naturally, everyone wanted to be his friend.

Little by little, the kids started picking up some of Kevin's good habits. After a while, it wasn't surprising to hear Darryl or Susie or Raymond say, "You look great today!" or "I like your new shoes."

Mrs. Timmons saw big changes in her classroom. She actually looked forward to coming to school.

One day, Mrs. Timmons was in the teachers lounge. Some of the other teachers were there, and one of them asked Mrs. Timmons how her class was doing. This time, she was able to say, "Oh, they are wonderful. They are so kind to each other!"

One teacher said, "It must have been my suggestion of rewarding them. It worked, didn't it?"

"No," said Mrs. Timmons, "that didn't work."

"Then it must have been my suggestion of punishing them that worked," said another teacher.

"No," said Mrs. Timmons, "that didn't work, either."

"Well, what was it that changed them?" all the teachers wanted to know.

"I found a secret weapon...and his name is Kevin!" smiled Mrs. Timmons.

Discuss the story by asking the following questions:

"How could Kevin's behavior change a whole class?" *(He was so pleasant that it made the other kids feel good to be around him. They wanted to be like him. Make the point that even one person performing acts of kindness can start a ripple effect and have a good influence on others.)*

"Have you ever watched the news and heard about senseless acts of violence?" *(Most, if not all, of the students will be able to answer, "Yes." Explain that these acts are random and that the victim often is no one the attacker even knows.)*

 Tell the students:

"Many people are tired of these senseless acts of violence, and there has been a campaign in our country to spread kindness, not violence. In this campaign, people are encouraging others to perform *random acts of kindness.* This means they might help someone get something off a top shelf at the grocery store, let someone you don't even know go ahead of you in line at the movies, open doors, and generally treat others with respect. The people who do these things are not expecting thanks or recognition."

Ask the students:

"What do you think the world would be like if there were only kindness?" *(Accept any appropriate answers.)*

"What do you think it would be like to come to school every day and know that you would be treated only with kindness?" *(Accept any appropriate answers.)*

 Have the students brainstorm about ways they can perform *random acts of kindness.* Some of their suggestions may be:

- Send letters or cards to sick children in the hospital.
- Have the class go to younger students' classrooms and help the children read.
- When walking through the halls at school, be friendly to people you don't even know.

When the students have finished brainstorming, show them the *Friendship Box.* Tell the students to write on a piece of paper acts of kindness they see their classmates performing and put the papers into the *Friendship Box.* The box will be opened once a week and the papers will be read. Tell the students they must identify the person who performed the act of kindness, but they may choose not to sign their own names.

---

5 **Activity:** Tell the class members you are going to give them their first opportunity to make someone in their classroom feel good. Have everyone write his or her name on a slip of paper. Collect the slips and put them in a container. Have each child draw a name, making sure no one draws his or her own name. Tell the students not to reveal whose name they have drawn. Emphasize the importance of keeping the name a secret. Distribute the *Friendship Worksheet* and a pencil to each student and have the students complete the worksheet as positively as possible. Tell the students not to write their own names on the sheet. Collect the sheets and give them to the people about whom they are written. If there is any concern that some students may have difficulty being kind, review the completed sheets before handing them out.

6 **Alternate Activity:** Have each student draw a name to determine who will be his or her *Secret Pal. (It can be the person from the previous activity, or the students can draw a different name.)* Have the students perform special kind acts for their *Secret Pals* for a week or two. At the end of the time period, reveal the identity of the *Secret Pals.* This activity can be repeated at various times throughout the school year.

7 Conclude the lesson by asking the students:

"What was it like having a classroom full of kindness?" *(Accept any appropriate answers.)*

FRIENDSHIP WORKSHEET

Name of Person I Chose_____

ADJECTIVES (#1)—CHOOSE FIVE ADJECTIVES THAT DESCRIBE THE PERSON ABOVE.

kind	dependable	funny	nice
friendly	cool	happy	generous
athletic	creative	helpful	talented
smiling	friendly	likable	thoughtful
artistic	responsible	lively	understanding
caring	exciting	musical	smart
cheerful	fun	neat	hard-working

NOUNS (#2)—CHOOSE TWO NOUNS THAT DESCRIBE THE PERSON ABOVE.

friend	boy	girl	person

PREDICATES (#3)—CHOOSE FIVE PREDICATES THAT DESCRIBE THE PERSON ABOVE.

is nice	learns quickly
works hard	has a good sense of humor
does well in school	is a good friend
cares about others	cooperates in school
gets along well with others	is a good sport
is fun to be with	is good at _____
has good ideas	is great at _____

FRIENDSHIP SENTENCE

Write a sentence that describes this person. Use the words circled above.

You are a/an _____ and _____ _____
                ADJECTIVE (#1)   ADJECTIVE (#1)   NOUN (#2)

who _____ and _____ .
                   PREDICATE (#3)   PREDICATE (#3)

THE NEIGHBORHOOD
A Lesson on Caring about Others

Note: This story and lesson may be used as a motivational beginning to a school-service project. School-service experiences are important in the development of children, if our goal is to have them grow up to be caring adults who reach out and help others.

MATERIALS NEEDED:

✔ Piece of construction paper, pencil, and scissors for each student

LESSON:

The facilitator should:

 Tell the class that you are going to tell a story about a girl who helped others. Then read or tell the following story:

> **Kendra Turner is in fourth grade. She lives with her mom and dog in a little house in a quiet neighborhood. Most of Kendra's friends are from school—not from her neighborhood—because there aren't any kids who live on her street. In fact, it was Kendra's opinion that she lived on the worst street in the world, because not only were there no kids, but the only people living there—besides Kendra and her mom—were really old. There was nothing to do at all.**
>
> **Mrs. Benson, the lady next door, was really old. Some of Kendra's friends from school were scared of Mrs. Benson because she looked so wrinkled and old and she was kind of crabby. Kendra wasn't scared of Mrs. Benson, but she did steer clear of her, because she had had a couple of bad experiences with her. Once her basketball had rolled into Mrs. Benson's yard and crushed some flowers. Mrs. Benson came out and yelled at Kendra. Another time, Kendra's dog, Muffin, got into Mrs. Benson's yard. Mrs. Benson came out of her house, threw a shoe at Muffin, and yelled for Kendra to come get her "mutt."**
>
> **Most of the time, Kendra was bored when she was at home. She stayed inside most of the time, avoiding Mrs. Benson. She wanted someone to play with so badly that she asked her mom if they could move to a different neighborhood, but her mom said they couldn't afford to do that. So Kendra resigned herself to being bored. Unless she invited a friend from school to come play with her, on weekdays she usually**

came home, watched TV, did homework, and went to bed. She stayed inside on the weekends, too, and watched a lot of TV.

One day, Kendra saw a program about kids. The reporter was interviewing people who said that kids nowadays are lazy and think only of themselves. That made Kendra mad. She knew that she wasn't lazy. She knew she cared about others, and she was going to prove it!

She went outside and looked around. She noticed that Mrs. Benson's yard was full of leaves, so she decided to rake them.

Mrs. Benson saw that Kendra was raking and came out of her house and yelled, "What are you doing?"

Kendra said, "I just thought that I would like to help you. I guess I should have asked first."

"If you think you're getting paid, you are wrong! I don't have any money," yelled the old lady.

"No ma'am, I didn't expect to get paid. I just wanted to help you," Kendra answered.

Mrs. Benson looked at Kendra for a minute. Then her face broke into a big smile. "Thank you," she said quite sweetly. Kendra couldn't believe what she saw and heard, and she felt wonderful and warm inside!

As Kendra raked the leaves, Mrs. Benson stayed outside and talked with her. She realized that the old lady wasn't really crabby at all. In fact, she was pretty nice. She told Kendra all about her children, who were grown and lived across the country. Since Kendra had never seen Mrs. Benson's children, she didn't think they came to visit their mom very often. That made Kendra feel sad for her neighbor. She thought that the old lady was probably very lonely. She stayed and talked with Mrs. Benson long after the leaves were raked and bagged.

That day was the beginning of many new experiences in Kendra's life. She realized that there were lots of lonely old people in her neighborhood and that most of them could use some help. Almost every day after school, Kendra would go to a neighbor's house and offer to help. She ran errands, got groceries, and sometimes just visited with people who were lonely. In no time, Kendra was busy every day. She certainly didn't have time to be bored!

Kendra's neighbors were poor, so she wasn't getting paid in money, but her payment was the good feeling she was getting from helping others.

One day, Mrs. Benson called Kendra and asked her if she could come over for a moment. Kendra thought the old lady needed some help, and she said, "I will be right there."

When Kendra got to Mrs. Benson's, she saw that many of the neighbors were in the living room. Mrs. Benson said, "Kendra, you know that none of us has very much money, but we want you to know how much we appreciate you, so we all decided to look around our houses and see what we could find that you might like. You know that I have a grown-up daughter who lives in California. Well, this was hers, and she doesn't need it anymore."

Kendra saw a faded blue bike. It was rusty and old, but Mrs. Benson was beaming and proud.

Then Mr. Sherman said, "This was my son's, but I would like to give it to you." He held out a beat-up baseball glove.

Mrs. Levy said, "My grandchildren are grown now, but they used to love this. I want you to have it," she pointed to a sled with one runner.

As she looked from the old wrinkled faces with big smiles to all the prized possessions they were offering to her, Kendra suddenly knew what caring and giving were all about.

She smiled and said, "Thank you! These are the best gifts I have ever received!"

 Discuss the story by asking the following questions:

"Why did Kendra begin helping her neighbors?" *(She was bored, and she was mad at the news report.)*

"After she got started, why did Kendra enjoy helping?" *(It made her feel good about herself.)*

"Were the gifts the old people offered Kendra valuable?" *(Not in money, but special to them because of memories. They were giving her very special gifts.)*

"Was Kendra lying at the end of the story when she said that the gifts were the best she had ever received?" *(No, because she knew how much they meant to the old people who gave them to her.)*

"When you give to others, do you always receive something back?" *(You don't always get money or a gift, but you do receive a good feeling.)*

Lively Lessons

3. Suggest to the class that it would be nice for them to experience the feeling that Kendra experienced when she helped the people in her neighborhood. Ask:

"How many of you would like to join a helping campaign?" *(Take a vote. Hopefully, everyone in the class will want to join.)*

"Why would you want to help others?" *(Because people really need help, and kindness will be repaid with good feeling.)*

4. Have the students brainstorm about some ideas for a class or school project. The project will be taken more seriously if it is suggested by the students. Guide the discussion and encourage the class to choose a realistic project. Some ideas might be:

- donating old toys to a children's home or to poor families during the holidays.
- collecting canned goods for a food bank.
- visiting a nursing home to sing for the residents.
- making cards for children who are in the hospital.

5. Have the class make a plan and set some goals. Delegate responsibilities so that the children are doing the work. Write a letter to parents, communicating the objectives that might be accomplished by working on the project. If possible, get every class in the school interested and make this a whole-school effort. Or have each class choose its own project.

6. **Activity:** Distribute a piece of construction paper, a pencil, and scissors to each student. Tell the students to trace one of their hands on the paper, write inside the outline what was done to help someone else, and cut out the hand. Have the students hang their completed hands on the classroom wall.

7. Conclude the lesson by recognizing the efforts made by the students. Contact the local newspaper to see if the editor would be interested in publishing a human-interest story about the positive deeds the students have performed.

THE GIFT
A Lesson on Cooperation

MATERIALS NEEDED:

✔ List of groups to which students in the class might belong. Some examples might be: a family, a classroom (also all the other classrooms in the school they might go to), a sports team (name all the different sports teams separately), Girl Scouts or Boy Scouts, 4-H Clubs, etc.

✔ Several index cards, each with the name of a simple machine or appliance (do not use *washing machine*.) written on it. Examples might be: soda machine, can opener, popcorn popper, lawn mower, sprinkler, etc.

✔ Art paper, pencils, and crayons or markers for each student group (optional)

LESSON:

The facilitator should:

 Greet the class and ask:

> "What do a family and a class have in common?" *(Both are groups of people who work and play together—sometimes happily, sometimes not so happily!)*

> "There are lots of groups in your life right now, and there will always be lots of groups. Can you name some different groups to which you belong or have belonged?" *(Scouts, orchestras, religious groups, special class groups, etc.)*

 Activity: Take your list of groups and say to the class:

> "Let's see how many groups you belong to now. Every time I name a group that you are a part of, stand up. Then sit down until you hear me name another group you are a part of."

If the groups are named fairly quickly, the students will be bouncing up and down and will understand the concept that everyone participates in groups throughout life.

 Tell the class:

> "Since everyone belongs to so many different groups, it would be nice if everyone got along and worked well together all the time. Unfortunately, some people seem to have trouble working with others. In fact, I want to tell you a story about a classroom that was not pleasant to be in at all."

Read or tell the following story:

There was a (<u>GRADE LEVEL TO WHICH THE STORY IS BEING PRESENTED</u>) grade class in Evans School that had a big problem. The teacher, Mrs. Rollins, is a great teacher, so the problem had nothing to do with her. It was the kids in the class. They just couldn't seem to get along, especially whenever Mrs. Rollins asked them to work in groups. When working together, she always heard comments such as, "No, do it *this* way!" or "I think that is a dumb idea!" or "I don't want to be in your group!" The kids in the class just couldn't seem to agree. Poor Mrs. Rollins got so tired of all their fighting that she just gave up on the idea of ever having them work together. She put the desks in rows and gave individual work assignments, because that was the only way she and the class had any peace.

One day, a girl named Karen heard that Mrs. Rollins' birthday was coming up. At recess, Karen called all her classmates together.

"Hey, guys, listen!" said Karen. "Mrs. Rollins' birthday is this Saturday. I heard her talking to Mrs. Peterson in the hall. I think we should give her a party!"

Carlos was very enthusiastic, "Great! Why don't we have a pizza party?"

Teisha said, "No, Mrs. Rollins likes sweet things better. She told me she has a real sweet tooth. I think we should have an ice-cream party!"

Carlos wrinkled up his face and said, "That's a really stupid idea! The ice cream would melt because we have nowhere to keep it cold."

Then the fighting began. Some kids wanted pizza, some wanted ice cream, and some had totally different ideas about what kind of food to serve. Everyone had a definite opinion, and everyone began to talk at once. No one could even hear what anyone else was saying, much less agree on what kind of food to serve at the party.

Karen said, "Well, maybe we could decide that part later. When should we have the party, since her birthday is on Saturday? I think it is better to surprise her ahead of time and have it on Friday."

"No," said Andrew, "I think it would surprise her more if it were on Monday. She really wouldn't be expecting that at all."

"Well, I don't think we *should* surprise her," interrupted Maria. "We'd better ask permission to have it!"

"You are so dumb!" said Peter.

"I am not dumb! You are!" Maria yelled back at Peter.

Before you knew it, the class was arguing at the top of its lungs. As usual, no one listened to anyone else. In fact, no one even heard Mrs. Rollins come out onto the playground to blow the whistle to signal the end of recess. Mrs. Rollins approached the group huddled on the playground and blew the whistle sharply, which startled them all into silence.

"What are you fighting about now?" Mrs. Rollins asked.

"Nothing," said Carlos, looking down at the ground.

"We are not going in until you tell me, so you'd better just tell the truth," Mrs. Rollins said sternly.

"Well, we were just planning a birthday party for you," said Karen in a very embarrassed voice.

Mrs. Rollins shook her head slowly, sighed, and said, "Class, let's go in and talk about this."

When the students were back in the classroom, Mrs. Rollins closed the door and said in a patient, kind voice, "Listen, I really appreciate the thought that you were trying to plan a party, but you don't do well when you try to work together. In fact, you don't seem to like each other very much at all, so I really don't think we would even enjoy a party. Let's not have any parties this year, all right? Now let's get back to work."

The students looked at each other. They knew that Mrs. Rollins was right. They could never get along well enough to plan any kind of party. There were just too many people with definite opinions in Mrs. Rollins' classroom.

One day about a week later, the students came into the room and saw a substitute teacher sitting at Mrs. Rollins' desk.

"Where is Mrs. Rollins?" asked Andrew. "Is she sick?"

"Everyone, sit down and I will tell you," said the substitute, Mr. Clamen.

When everyone was seated, Mr. Clamen said, "I am sorry to tell you that Mrs. Rollins had an accident last night. She fell down the steps at her home and broke her leg. It seems that it is a bad break and she must stay in the hospital for a while. If you all want to make some cards for her, I will take them to her in the hospital."

Everyone in the class felt terrible. Mrs. Rollins was a nice teacher and her students really cared for her.

At recess, Karen called everyone together. "Hey, guys," she said, "let's make something for Mrs. Rollins to show her that we are thinking about her. If we can work on it together, it will show her that we are really trying to get along."

"That's a great idea!" said Carlos. "Why don't we buy a T-shirt? We can all sign it for her."

"That is the stupidest idea I ever heard," said Teisha. "She is not going to wear a T-shirt in the hospital! I think we should make her a big card that everyone can sign."

"No," said Andrew, "I think we should..."

"STOP IT!" yelled Paula, a shy girl, who usually didn't talk much.

Everyone stopped and stared at her. Paula's cheeks were bright red, and she looked just as surprised as everyone else that she had yelled. Paula said, "You are all doing what we always do in this class, and that is argue. Let's really try to get along for Mrs. Rollins' sake. I will go and get a piece of paper and I will write down everyone's ideas. We can vote to see whose idea wins. But we all have to agree right now that whichever idea wins is the idea we will go with."

The kids thought that Paula's idea was great, so she ran in and got a sheet of paper to write ideas on. There were eight ideas, including Carlos' T-shirt idea and Teisha's big card. Everyone voted, and the idea that won by one vote was to make a big mural for Mrs. Rollins' hospital room.

Then Andrew said, "Let's use paint and make it real bright!"

Karen said, "No, paint is too messy. I think we should just use our crayons."

Andrew started to open his mouth to argue, then looked at Paula. He took a deep breath and said calmly, "How about using markers? They are less messy, and there are bright colors!"

Everyone agreed that markers would be best to use. Then the discussion turned to what the subject of the mural should be. Karen suggested that they each draw themselves, but Carlos disagreed.

"I think we should draw the scenery outside our classroom window, so that Mrs. Rollins will feel that she is looking out the *classroom* window instead of the *hospital* window," said Carlos.

Suddenly, they looked at each other and said in unison, "We could do both!" Paula asked if that was all right with everyone. Everyone nodded in agreement. It was the first time they had agreed on anything!

The class worked on the picture for the rest of the day. They worked together as a team and, in the end, they all agreed that it was the most gorgeous mural any of them had ever seen.

Mr. Clamen, the substitute teacher, took that mural to Mrs. Rollins and she LOVED it! First, because it really was a pretty, bright mural. And second, as unbelievable as it seemed to her, she knew that all the students in her class had worked on it together.

Mrs. Rollins came back to school about one week later. She had to walk on crutches, but it was a very happy day. She and her class celebrated by having a party. They had pizza, followed by ice cream!

 Discuss the story by asking the students the following questions:

"What word describes when people work peacefully together as a group?" (Cooperation. *You can draw blanks on the board and play* Wheel of Fortune *until they guess the word, if they don't know it right away.*)

"Why did Mrs. Rollins' class not know how to cooperate?" *(They could not get along, because everyone wanted his/her own way and would not accept anyone else's suggestions.)*

"If people are going to cooperate, they have to agree to agree. What does that mean?" *(People must agree in advance that they will find an answer that can and will satisfy everyone.)*

 Tell the students:

"Once people decide to agree to agree, they sometimes have to compromise. They may compromise by voting, settling on something quite different, or meeting in the middle. Groups often have leaders, but that does not mean that the leader is the boss. Everyone should have a say, even though that doesn't mean everyone can always have his or her way. When people enjoy the work and work together, they get more done."

 Activity: Divide the class into groups of four. Then tell the class:

"Today we are going to see if this class can work in small groups and cooperate.

I will give each group an index card with the name of an appliance or simple machine written on it. What is written on your card is a secret. Only your group members may know what it is. For example: If *Washing Machine* is written on your card, three students can hold hands to form a circle. Another student can then stand in the middle and twist back and forth to show agitating movement." *(Have a group of students demonstrate the washing machine.)* "Your task is to somehow act out for the whole class the movement of what is written on the index card. It is important that each group get to perform until its act is over, even if the answer is obvious. The class members have the job of guessing what their actions represent, but may not guess until the act has ended. The rules are that everyone must have a part and must cooperate while planning. You will have about 10 minutes to plan your actions. After you have performed your act and the class has guessed the name of the machine, I will ask you to tell how you cooperated, whether there were any problems, and how you settled any disputes."

Alternate Activity #2: Divide the class into groups. Give each group one marker and a large piece of paper. Have each group draw pictures of things that are the color of the marker the group was given. The number of things drawn by each group should equal one less than the number of members in the group. For example: If a group of four children has a brown marker, group members may draw three things that are brown. They must cooperate and be fair about what they decide to draw and who draws it. Everyone must have a part.

When the groups have finished drawing, have each one explain the method used and how group members made sure they were fair.

8 **Alternate Activity #3:** Divide the class into groups. Give each group a large piece of paper and a box of crayons. Assign each group a place, such as zoo, grocery store, toy store, park, kitchen, or department store. Tell each group to draw pictures of things that can be found in the place assigned to that group. The number of things drawn by each group should equal one less than the number of members in the group. For example: If the group has four members, they can draw only three things. When the drawings are complete, have each group show its drawings to the class and discuss how group members agreed on what to draw.

9 Teach children the following rap:

We can learn to work and play without one single fight.
If we try to get along, then everything's all right!

We may have to compromise or sometimes even vote,
But when we cooperate, no one ever needs to gloat.

Conclude the lesson by reminding the class that the children in the story did not enjoy each other until they learned to cooperate. Challenge the students to find new ways to get along, work together, and enjoy each other. Tell the students that you will be checking in on their progress and that you would love hearing good news from their teacher!

WHATEVER
A Lesson on the Importance of Expressing Feelings

MATERIALS NEEDED:

✔ Puppet
✔ Paper and pencil for each student
✔ Chalkboard and chalk
✔ Poster with "I Message" format
  Example: "I feel _____ because _____ ." When talking with a person you have a problem with, add what you would like that person to do. "I feel _____ because you _____ and I would like you to please _____ ."
✔ Copy of *Feelings Rap* (page 61) for each student

LESSON:

The facilitator should:

Distribute a piece of paper and a pencil to each student. Greet the students and use a puppet to focus the students' attention. Have the puppet act shy and whisper in your ear. Tell the students what the puppet says in the following conversation:

Facilitator: "How are you feeling today?"
Puppet: "I am exuberant today! But I was feeling a little apprehensive yesterday because of a test *(or weather, if it is appropriate)*."
Facilitator: "My friend certainly has a good vocabulary. Does anyone know what the words *exuberant* and *apprehensive* mean?"

Allow time for answers. Clarify the definitions, if necessary. Then tell the students:

"It is good to have a big vocabulary of feeling words. There are a multitude of feeling words, some of which you may never have heard. For example, does anyone know what *livid* or *remorseful* means? *(Allow time for answers.)* I want you to take your papers and pencils and list as many feeling words as you can in five minutes." *(Or whatever time restrictions you care to make.)*

When the students have completed their lists, brainstorm about the feeling words they have listed. Write the words on the chalkboard. On the next page, is an example of a word list from a fifth-grade lesson:

afraid	aggravated	amazed	angry
anxious	apprehensive	astonished	awkward
bashful	bored	brave	cheerful
confident	confused	curious	delighted
depressed	disappointed	discouraged	distressed
down	ecstatic	embarrassed	excited
exuberant	fearful	fearless	frightened
frustrated	furious	giddy	glad
gleeful	gloomy	good	grumpy
guilty	happy	hurt	impatient
irritated	jealous	jolly	joyful
jubilant	jumpy	livid	lonely
loved	mad	merry	miserable
nervous	panicky	peaceful	pressured
proud	quiet	relaxed	relieved
remorseful	sad	scared	sensitive
shocked	shy	silly	sorry
stressed	surprised	tense	terrified
thankful	ticked off	upset	uptight
woeful	worried		

After writing the word list on the chalkboard, discuss the following points:

- All humans experience every one of these feelings, but we don't always know the word to describe what we are feeling.
- Some of these feelings are comfortable and some are uncomfortable. Some feelings we like having and some we don't, but all feelings are part of life. *(If desired, you may categorize words for comfortable and uncomfortable feelings.)*
- Feelings originate in the brain, but we often feel symptoms of them in other parts of our body. Some people have physical problems, such as upset stomachs or headaches, when they don't properly deal with uncomfortable feelings.

 Read or tell the following story:

*(Optional: When telling this story, let the class guess Jerry's underlined feelings. Tell them to say "**Whatever**" in unison whenever they see you shrug your shoulders.)*

When Jerry was a little boy, he expressed his feelings like most little kids do. When he was sad, he cried; when he was mad, he yelled; and when he was happy, he would laugh and smile. That was when he was little.

Now he is in (<u>GRADE LEVEL TO WHICH THE STORY IS BEING PRESENTED</u>**) grade. Somewhere between then and now, Jerry has developed the idea that it is "uncool" to show his feelings. And Jerry wants to be the "coolest."**

So now when he is sad, Jerry carefully masks his face and simply says, *(Shrug your shoulders and continue to do so whenever the word "**Whatever**" appears in the story.)* **"Whatever."**

When he is mad, he masks his face and he says, "Whatever."

When he is happy, his face remains blank and he says, "Whatever."

One day, Jerry was sitting in school. A big math test had been graded and returned. Jerry had really studied hard for that test, but his paper came back with a big red 62% written across the top. Inside, Jerry felt (<u>SAD, DISAPPOINTED, EMBARRASSED</u>**).** *(Let the kids guess the feelings that are underlined and, if necessary, add the feelings named in the story to what they have said.)* **But on the outside, Jerry kept his face calm, dismissively waved his hand, and said, "Whatever."**

Another day, one of the biggest bullies in the school grabbed Jerry's homework and tore it into shreds. On the inside, Jerry felt (<u>SAD, HUMILIATED, ANGRY, EMBARRASSED, OUTRAGED</u>**). On the outside, Jerry mockingly applauded and said, "Whatever."**

In gym one day, the class was playing soccer. The gym teacher appointed two captains to choose teams. Jerry was the last person chosen. On the inside, he felt (<u>EMBARRASSED, LEFT OUT, UNAPPRECIATED</u>). On the outside, he kept his face calm and said, "Whatever."

Jerry doesn't just use his "whatever" reaction at school. He uses it at home, too. One day, his mother greeted him at the door with the news that his grandmother had been in a car accident and was in the hospital. Jerry looked at her, said, "Whatever," and went to his room.

Jerry has pushed so many feelings down so often that he isn't even sure what his feelings *are* anymore. He just knows that he doesn't feel well and that he walks around all day with a knot in his stomach. At night, he doesn't usually sleep well, and he often wakes up feeling groggy and tired.

Jerry's mom noticed his unhappiness. In fact, a couple of times she said, "Jerry, I know something is wrong with you. Why don't you sit down and talk with me? Tell me what is wrong!"

But Jerry wouldn't do that. In fact, he *couldn't* do that anymore. He couldn't recognize the feelings he was having, much less be able to tell his mom about them.

One day, Jerry was on the way home from school when a teenager standing on the corner motioned him over. The teenager said, "Hey, kid, want to feel real good? I have some pills here that will make you feel great. I'm selling them really cheap today, five pills for five dollars."

Jerry had learned to say *no* to drugs just like all kids learn in school and from their parents. He was just about to say *No* when he thought about what the teenager said. He hesitated and asked, "What do you mean: I will feel real good?"

The boy said, "Oh, these are great! Take one and you will fly high all day. Everything will be great."

Jerry said, "And they are just five dollars? I have five dollars at home. All right, I will buy some from you. Can you be here tomorrow after school? I'll bring the money then."

"Sure," said the boy. "I will meet you tomorrow, same time, same place!"

As Jerry walked home, he thought, "Maybe this is just what I need."

When Jerry got home, his mom was waiting for him. She looked at him and said, "Jerry, what is the matter? Please sit down and talk with me."

Jerry said, "Mom, leave me alone. I am going up to my room." In his room, he counted out five one-dollar bills and put them on his dresser.

That night, Jerry had an extremely restless sleep. He tossed, turned, and dreamt all night. One of the dreams he had was very vivid. He dreamt that he met the little boy that he used to be. It was weird, talking to himself as a six-year-old kid. The little Jerry said, "You don't have to take pills to feel better. Why don't you just tell Mommy what is wrong with you? She always helps me feel better!"

Jerry said, "I don't even know what to say or how to explain what's wrong with me."

In the dream, six-year-old Jerry said, "If I can do it, you can, too!"

After that, Jerry sat up and rubbed his face. "Wow, that seemed real!" He didn't sleep any more that night, but lay in bed thinking about his dream.

In the morning, he slowly got dressed, put the five dollars in his pocket, and went downstairs to leave for school. His mom was alarmed to see how bad he looked. She said, "Please, Jerry, talk with me."

Jerry started to say, "Whatever," but he remembered the strange dream. He wondered if his mom *could* help him.

He decided to try to talk with her. "Well, Mom, I haven't been feeling too good lately. I feel kind of sick when I think about Grandma."

"You mean you are worried?" his mom asked.

Jerry thought about this. "Yeah," he said, "I guess I am!"

Mom asked Jerry what else he had been feeling. Words started tumbling forth. "Well, in school last week, I got a low grade on a math test and I felt so disappointed because I had really studied...and in gym they didn't pick me and I felt so embarrassed...and I felt mad when this kid tore up my homework paper...and...."

Words and emotions just started flowing. Jerry started to cry as he talked.

Mom sat there quietly and listened for an hour. During that hour that Jerry talked, a very funny thing started to happen: He felt *lighter*. He felt the knot in his stomach loosen. He knew he still had all the same problems, but he felt *different*. One feeling he recognized was *relief*.

Jerry's mom hugged him and said, "I am so glad that you shared all that with me. I want you to know that I will always listen to you and help you any way I can."

Jerry believed her. Later that day, he remembered that the teenager was going to be waiting for him on the corner. He started to walk a different way, but decided he might as well not avoid the kid. When the boy saw Jerry, he said, "I have your pills right here."

Jerry said, "No thanks, I have changed my mind."

The teenager said, "Is five dollars too much? I will give them to you cheaper. How about five pills for three dollars? That's really a deal."

Jerry shook his head.

"How about five pills for two dollars? Remember, they make you feel real good!"

Jerry said, "I found something that made me feel good and it's free." And he walked all the way home without looking back.

 Discuss the story by asking the students the following questions:

"Why did Jerry almost turn to drugs?" *(He was unhappy and upset and didn't know how to deal effectively with his problems.)*

"Do you think that this is why people sometimes turn to drugs?" *(Accept either* Yes *or* No *accompanied by an explanation.)*

"Are there other ways to express feelings besides talking?" *(Through art, music, writing)*

"Why is it good to know lots of 'feeling words'?" *(If you know lots of "feeling words," you will be able to describe exactly how you are feeling so others will understand.)*

"What are some good choices to make when you are experiencing uncomfortable feelings?" *(Getting help, expressing yourself, etc.)*

"What are some poor choices to make when you are experiencing uncomfortable feelings?" *(Violence, alcohol, drugs, keeping your feelings inside, etc.)*

Introduce "I Messages." Display the poster and tell the students that it is an excellent way to discuss feelings. Discuss the poster format, using some examples. Then have several students use the format. Examples can include:

- Someone calls you a name.
- You have a math test tomorrow.
- Your puppy is sick.

 Conclude the lesson by distributing a copy of the *Feelings Rap* to each student and reciting it as a group. When you have finished reciting the rap, tell the students to save their copies of the *Feelings Rap* for the next lesson, *Chester Chills.*

FEELINGS RAP

Happy, embarrassed, frustrated, mad,

Angry, nervous, impatient, sad,

Proud, scared, shy, bored,

Discouraged, excited, jealous, and more.

These are feelings that we've all had,

They're human emotions, neither good nor bad.

It's the choices we make and how we react

That make them a problem, and that's a fact!

CHESTER CHILLS
A Lesson on Stress

Note: Follows *Whatever* Story

MATERIALS NEEDED:

- ✔ Puppet
- ✔ *Feelings Rap* (page 61) from *Whatever* lesson
- ✔ 6" x 18" piece of construction paper, pencil, and crayons or markers for each student
- ✔ Chalkboard and chalk

LESSON:

The facilitator should:

 Greet the students and introduce the puppet by name. Then have the following conversation with the puppet:

> **Facilitator:** "Well, (<u>PUPPET'S NAME</u>) how are you feeling today?"
> **Puppet:** "Not so good. My older brother is leaving for a long trip, and I'm worried and upset."
> **Facilitator:** "I'm sorry to hear that, but I'm glad that you can talk about your feelings."

Remind the students that, in the previous lesson, the class talked about uncomfortable feelings and how these feelings are sometimes difficult to deal with. Then ask the students to take out their copies of the *Feelings Rap* from the last lesson and recite it together.

> Happy, embarrassed, frustrated, mad,
> Angry, nervous, impatient, sad,
> Proud, scared, shy, bored,
> Discouraged, excited, jealous, and more.
>
> These are feelings that we've all had,
> They're human emotions, neither good nor bad.
> It's the choices we make and how we react
> That make them a problem, and that's a fact!

 Tell the students that you are going to tell them a story about a boy who didn't know how to handle uncomfortable feelings. Then read or tell the following story:

When Chester was young, he was like any typical kid. He had fun, played games, and was happy most of the time.

But like any typical kid, sometimes Chester *wasn't* happy. He sometimes worried about things like his grades or storms or whether he was going to score a goal during his soccer game. He didn't like the worried feelings, so he usually talked things over with his mom, and that helped him feel better. Then things would go back to normal, the worried feeling would go away, and Chester would go back to being his happy, carefree self.

The year that Chester turned 10, his family had some hard times. His dad lost his job and his mom had to go to work. She seemed to be busy all of the time and didn't have time to talk with him as often as she had in the past. Chester really couldn't talk with his dad about things because his dad was so upset about being out of work.

That was the year that Chester's worries seemed to get out of hand. It seemed like he was worrying all the time about almost everything. He worried that when his mom went to her job, she might not come back. He worried at night that he might oversleep and be late for school. When he got to school on time, he worried that he might be late the *next* day. Chester worried constantly about his dad's job, and he worried that he was not growing enough. He worried every night that he wouldn't be able to sleep. Then he started worrying that he was worrying too much!

Naturally, all of this worrying had an effect on Chester. He felt tired, felt upset, and had headaches. Most the time, Chester walked around feeling like he had a knot in his stomach. He knew he had to get help from someone.

Chester went to his dad and told him how he felt. His dad said, "Try not to worry, Son." Chester really *tried* not to worry, but the worrying didn't stop.

Next, Chester went to his mom. She wanted to help him, but she really didn't know what to do. She hugged Chester and told him that everything would be better. Then she said that she had to leave for work. Chester didn't feel any better.

He decided to talk with one of his friends about his feelings. His friend said, "Just chill!" Well, Chester really *tried* to chill, but he didn't even know how to start.

He went to school and told his teacher about his nervous and worried feelings. She suggested that he see the school counselor, Mrs. Carlson.

So Chester made an appointment with the counselor. After listening to him, Mrs. Carlson said that it sounded like Chester's worrying was causing him a lot of stress. She thought it would be good for Chester to learn some ways to relax. She explained that learning how to relax wouldn't make the problems go away, but it *would* help him release his feelings of worry and make him feel better. Chester was so concerned about how he felt that he thought anything was worth a try. So he agreed to learn what Mrs. Carlson wanted to teach him.

Mrs. Carlson taught Chester some things he could do to unwind and relax when he started feeling worried and tense. As Chester learned these different techniques, he began to feel more at peace with himself and with the situations around him. In fact, he did such a good job of learning to manage his own stress that Mrs. Carlson has asked him to help other children who have the same problem.

Chester really did learn how to "CHILL!"

3. Discuss the story by asking the students the following questions:

"What is stress?" *(Stress is a buildup of uncomfortable feelings such as fear, anger, worry, etc. The feelings can build to a point where they can cause physical discomfort, such as headaches, stomachaches, and shortness of breath.)*

"What happened to Chester's body when he worried?" *(He felt tired, upset, had headaches, and walked around feeling like he had a knot in his stomach.)*

"Where do you feel tension in your body when you are scared, nervous, or worried?" *(Accept any appropriate answers. Point out that people are different and experience stress differently.)*

Explain that in primitive times, a person who experienced danger had an *adrenaline rush.* This rush of energy helped him/her to either fight or flee. But people today don't always discharge this energy by fighting or fleeing. Instead, they worry, and new problems can result if people don't learn to relax and handle the problems they must face.

4. Tell the students that you are going to teach them the techniques Chester's counselor taught him so that they, too, will have some ways to "chill."

Ask the students to describe how they "chill." Write their ideas on the chalkboard. When the list is complete, review the seven ideas listed on the next page, either pointing out how the students' ideas fit into one of the categories or introducing a non-mentioned category as another stress-reducing technique.

1. Relaxation

   Relaxing ideas include:
   — breathing deeply (from the diaphragm).
   — saying a calming word over and over.
   — tensing muscles throughout your body, then loosening them.
   — sitting back and looking at a peaceful scene—even imagining you are part of it.

2. Positive thinking and visualization

   Think thoughts such as: "I can do this" and picture yourself succeeding.

3. Staying healthy

   Eat healthy foods and get enough rest.

4. Exercising

   Note that exercise is very important, not just for general health, but because when we exercise, our body releases *endorphins*. (*Endorphins* are calming hormones.)

5. Recreation

   Having fun is important. Develop hobbies that you can pursue now and can continue to enjoy when you are older. Look beyond TV and video games!

6. Changing what you can!

   Reduce stress by setting goals, using time wisely, and problem-solving. Make changes to reduce the stress within you. For example, if you are always nervous because you lose things, set a goal to become organized.

7. Expressing your feelings

   Talk and use "I Messages." Express yourself through writing in journals, art, and music. A pet can be a great listener, too!

 Activity: Have the students make their own booklets. Distribute a piece of construction paper, a pencil, and crayons or markers to each student. Have the students fold the construction paper in half and then in half again to form a booklet. On the front of the booklet, have the students design a cover. For example, a student might draw a picture of him/herself and call the book "How to Chill." On each page of the booklet, have the students write a word or two about ways to relax and illustrate the words they choose. Encourage hesitant artists to at least draw stick figures. Give them ideas, if needed, on how to make the drawings meaningful.

When the booklets are completed, encourage the students to take them home and share them with their families. Tell the students that these same ideas work for everyone. Grown-ups, too!

6 Conclude the lesson by reciting the following poem:

Chester chilled and you can, too,
If you learn some simple things to do.

When you get stressed and all upset,
Relax yourself, breathe deeply, don't fret!

Think nice thoughts, jump and run.
Start some hobbies, have some fun.

Eat good foods, get some rest,
And your feelings do express.

Change the things under your control.
Dream some dreams, take the starring role.

If you follow these steps, as a rule,
Stress will fade, and you'll keep your cool!

Lively Lessons

SEEING DOUBLE!
A Lesson on Study Skills

MATERIALS NEEDED:

✔ Copy of *Proofreading* (page 73) and a red pen or pencil for each student

LESSON:

The facilitator should:

 Greet the students and ask:

"Who wants to improve his or her grades?" *(Most students will raise their hands.)*

Then say:

"Well, you are in luck today! That's what we are going to talk about, and I want to start by telling you a story."

 Read or tell the following story:

Tim and Tom are 10–year–old identical twins. They look alike, they talk alike, and they like a lot of the same things, such as eating hot dogs, collecting baseball cards, and playing video games. But there is one major way they differ, and that is in the kind of students they are.

You see, Tim is a very good student. He gets good grades because he works hard at his job. He has great study habits. *(Have the students tell you what they think his good study habits are. You can add anything they don't say, or you can continue reading.)* **Tim is organized at home and at school and in between! Tim's desks at school and at home are very neat. He knows where everything is, and he always has the supplies he needs where he needs them. At school, he keeps an assignment book in which he writes down all his assignments. He checks it every day before he leaves school and always makes sure he has all the books he will need for his homework. He writes long–term assignments on a calendar. He plans how long each part of the assignment will take, so he will finish the work on time.**

Tim usually likes to do his homework as soon as he gets home from school. He sits at his desk in a quiet room with no distractions. He works at a steady pace. He doesn't rush, and he doesn't daydream between sentences or problems. When his work is finished, he checks his paper

carefully, puts it in his "Back to School" Folder, puts the folder in his bookbag, and hangs his bookbag on the door to his room. Then—and only then—he relaxes, watches TV, or plays video games until dinner time.

Tom is quite a different story! First of all, he is a complete slob! (*Have the class, if you like, help on this part of the story by telling what a slob would do.*) Tom's desk at school is messy. His papers get wrinkled because he never uses folders. Tom just kind of shoves everything into his desk during the school day. At the end of the day, sometimes he remembers to take his books and papers home. Sometimes he doesn't. He never writes down assignments and he doesn't usually remember whether he even *has* any assignments. He almost never has book reports to turn in, because he forgets assignments made weeks before they are due. If he does his homework at all, he does it right before going to bed, after his mom has nagged him all evening to do it. He works while lying on the bed, with music playing and the television blaring. You can imagine what his grades are like!

But, as I told you, other than this major difference, Tom and Tim are very much alike. They love being twins! One evening, when they were sitting at the dinner table with their mom and dad, they told their parents how they had played a trick on one of their friends. Alex had come over to the boys' house and asked for Tim. Well, Tom had gone outside and was able to fool Alex into thinking *he* was Tim! The boys laughed and said, "We could fool anybody if we wanted! It is so cool to be twins!"

The boys' mom looked at them and said, "You could never fool me. All I would ever have to do is watch you do your homework for about 30 seconds and I could tell who is Tom and who is Tim!"

Tom said, "We could fool you if we wanted to!"

Tim agreed.

Their mom said, "Okay, we will make a bet! If you can fool me for one week, I will take you both to the amusement park for one last time this year. But remember, I must not be able to tell the difference between you two."

"Really, Mom? The amusement park?" asked Tim.

"Sure!" said their mom.

"Okay, it's a deal!" And the boys ran into their room to plan how they were going to fool their mother.

Tom said, "Mom will be able to tell us apart if we keep doing our homework the way we usually do. So maybe for a week you should do your homework like I do."

Tim said, "NO WAY! I don't want to get your grades! And if we just exchanged the way we do our work, Mom would expect that. The only thing is for you to do your work like I do for one week."

Tom groaned, "That's a lot of work. You never have any fun!"

"That's just too bad. If you want to go to the amusement park, you have to do it!" said Tim.

"Okay, okay, how do I do this?" asked Tom.

Tim spent the next half hour teaching Tom some good study habits. He told Tom that he would have to clean his desk at school, just in case their mom peeked in during the day, clean his desk at home, use an assignment book and folders, and do all the rest of the things Tim does. Tom thought he would never be able to do it all, but he sure wanted to fool their mom.

Monday was the day Tim and Tom started the plan. They dressed exactly alike and were very careful not to do anything that would give them away. That night, both boys came straight in from school, sat at their desks, and began their homework. All evening, their mom kept trying to sneak up and see the difference in their schoolwork, but Tom was very careful to proofread and do his work neatly. Their mom COULD NOT see any difference in their work!

Tuesday morning, Tom said that he would never be able to keep it up. But Tim, acting as a cheerleader, said, "Come on, you can do it. It is only for one week! Please, I really want to go to the amusement park!"

Tom said, "All right, but this is torture!"

Tuesday evening, Mom kept sneaking in to see what the boys were doing, but once again she COULD NOT tell the difference. She admitted that she was very surprised that Tom was able to keep this up. She was sure that he would start being lazy and then she would be able to tell who was Tom and who was Tim.

On Wednesday, Tom was still complaining privately to Tim. But he was really starting to get the hang of what he called "all this study stuff." So far, the boys had been able to make their plan work.

Thursday came, and their mom *still* couldn't tell who was who. And something else remarkable started happening: Tom's grades were coming up! For almost a week, he had proofread and turned in every assignment on time and the effects were starting to show.

Finally, Friday arrived. For a whole week, Tom had done everything the same way as a person with good study skills. He even forgot to complain!

On Friday afternoon, the boys' mom met them after school and said, "Well, I didn't think you could do it. I am totally confused! I don't know which one of you is Tom and which one is Tim. You did it!"

They both shouted together, "YES!!!!! Are we really going to the amusement park?"

Mom answered, "A deal is a deal. We will go tomorrow!"

Tim and Tom had a great time. They went on all the cool rides and had a blast! But you know what? Something else happened after that day. Tom realized that trying hard in school and using good study habits wasn't as bad as he had thought it was going to be. He actually *enjoyed* getting better grades. So after that "week of torture," he kept being organized, using good study habits, and "getting his act together."

But it was Tom and Tim's mom who had the last laugh. About a week later, she was on the phone talking with her sister, the boys' aunt. She said, "I played the best trick on Tom and Tim! They think that they fooled me, but I can always tell the difference between them. Tom has a freckle on his nose that Tim doesn't have. I just let them think they fooled me because I wanted Tom's study habits to improve. And do you know what? IT WORKED!"

 Discuss the story by asking the following questions:

"At the beginning of the story, why were Tim's grades better than Tom's?" *(Tim's materials were organized, at home and at school, because:*

- *Tim used an assignment book.*
- *Tim used folders and a bookbag to help him organize his materials.*
- *Tim had an organized system of doing his work.*
- *Tim made sure he had the books he needed at home in the evening.*
- *Tim showed self-discipline by doing his work before playing.*
- *Tim concentrated when he did his work.*
- *Tim proofread his work.*
- *Tim used his time wisely and planned ahead.*
- *Tim made his best effort.*
- *Tom did none of these things and didn't seem to care!)*

"Tom's mom tricked him because she knew his grades would improve if he took a little more care in doing his work. Do you think his grades would improve if he turned in even one extra assignment?" *(Accept any appropriate answers.)*

"How do teachers average grades?" *(After a few answers, show the class how to average grades. Use five grades. Make them 80's and 90's. Then say that one of those papers was not turned in. Average the grades with one zero. Then do it with two zeros.)*

"Now do you think each assignment is important when the teacher is figuring your grade average?" *(Yes.)*

4 Discuss how using good study habits, proofreading, and being consistent could improve a student's grades. Explain that although proofreading is a very good habit to get into, many students do not take the time to do it. Ask the students:

"If you stopped to proofread, what would you find on your papers?" *(Mistakes)*

"If you find mistakes, what can you do with them?" *(Correct the mistakes)*

"If you don't proofread, who finds the mistakes?" *(Teacher)*

"What does the teacher do with mistakes?" *(Counts them wrong)*

"Is proofreading guaranteed to raise your grades?" *(If done conscientiously, yes)*

5 Distribute a copy of *Proofreading* and a red pencil or pen to each student. Review the directions and have the students make the corrections. When the students have finished proofreading, have them correct their own papers.

6 Discuss the following study habits. Each study habit can be dealt with briefly in this lesson or in a supplementary lesson presented at a later date.

ORGANIZATION—Tell the students:

"*Organization* is more than keeping your desk clean. Along with the organization of materials, an organized person has a system of doing things that prevents him or her from forgetting what needs to be done. Some ways to be organized are to use folders, assignment sheets or books, calendars, binders, and/ or bookbags or backpacks. How do you think these things help a person stay organized?" *(They give a person the tools to stay organized. For example, if you know your homework is always in your homework folder, you will never have to hunt for it.)*

Finish this topic by having the students "organize" their desks and binders.

USING TIME WISELY—Say to the students:

"We are going to see if you know how long a minute is by playing a short game. Put your heads down on your desks. When I say go, I will start timing for one minute. When you think the minute is up, raise your hand."

Go on to explain that even though a minute seemed like a long time in the game, there are only so many minutes in a day. Ask the following questions:

"How many seconds are in a minute?" *(60)*

"How many minutes in an hour?" *(60)*

"How many hours in a day?" *(24)*

"How many minutes in a day?" *(1,440)*

"How do you think some students waste many of those minutes during a school day?" *(They might be:*

- *sharpening pencils during work time.*
- *getting numerous drinks of water.*
- *dawdling in the restroom.*
- *talking with friends.*
- *looking for lost materials.*
- *daydreaming.*
- *dwelling on one hard problem.)*

"What are some ways students should use their minutes wisely?" *(They should:*

- *work during work time, then play.*
- *decide whether they prefer to do the hard tasks first or the easy ones. [Ask the students which they prefer, telling them that as long as they use a plan, either can work.]*
- *focus their attention.*
- *organize their materials so they can be found easily.*
- *save socializing for recess.*
- *not spend too much time on one question, but rather go on and then go back to it later.*
- *get a drink of water after the work is done.)*

 Conclude the lesson by reminding the students that they all raised hands when they were asked who wanted better grades. Now that they know how to earn them, it is time to get started!

As a final reminder, read the following poem:

Good study habits are easy to form,
And make a difference in your grades.
Start today, and make some changes now,
And on your report card, you'll get paid.

PROOFREADING

Directions: There are more than **2 5** errors in the following two paragraphs. Cross out the mistakes with a colored pencil or pen and make corrections above the words.

the proofreading story

sue is a forth grad girl who doesnt like prooread. she think she has all the answer write and doesnt want to tak the time to proof.

sues grades arent very Good and shE can get detter grads can you thenk of a Way sue can get better gredes

TYRONE THE CYCLONE
A Lesson on Organization

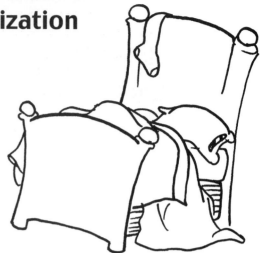

MATERIALS NEEDED:

✔ Copy of *Organization Skills* (page 79), construction paper, and a pencil for each student

LESSON:

The facilitator should:

 Greet the students and ask:

"Can any of you tell me what skill you could acquire that would have an effect not only on your success in school, but on your entire life?" *(Allow time for answers. When* organization *is mentioned, compliment the student who suggests it. If* organization *is not mentioned, tell the students that being organized is one skill that will benefit them throughout life.)*

Then say:

"*Organization* is the topic of today's lesson. If you listen and apply what you learn, you'll see how you can be more successful. We will start by listening to a story."

 Read or tell the following story:

Tyrone Johnson is in (<u>GRADE LEVEL TO WHICH THE STORY IS BEING PRESENTED</u>) grade and is a great kid. He has many friends and, if you ever met him, you would probably like him. He is helpful, friendly, good in sports, and polite to his mother.

However, Tyrone has one major problem. He is a total slob! *Disorganized* **is one term that teachers usually use to describe Tyrone, and his mother has a pet name for him. She calls him "Tyrone the Cyclone!"**

Tyrone's room at home looks like a cyclone hit it! Dirty clothes and clean clothes are piled in his room, and hopefully he knows which clothes are dirty and which ones are clean. When Tyrone takes his clothes off at night, he sometimes just tosses them anywhere. This explains why he has a sock and a T-shirt hanging from the ceiling light.

Tyrone collects all kinds of things, and the things he has collected are also laying around. Once, Tyrone's mom looked into his room and saw a big pile of leaves in the corner. She didn't even want to *ask* why they were there. Tyrone sometimes eats in his room. Once, when he had been eating pizza, a friend called and asked Tyrone if he could come over and play baseball. Tyrone laid the pizza on the dresser and forgot about it. A week later, it was still there, getting rather green and moldy. A quick look around the room showed other food items in various and assorted places.

Almost worse than the mess was the lack of organization. When getting dressed in the morning, it was really a challenge for Tyrone to find something to wear. He might have a pair of socks in two different drawers. His shirts were mixed in with his rock collection, and his shoes could be anywhere!

Tyrone was the same way at school. What do you think his desk looked like? *(If desired, the students can answer the question.)* His papers, crayons, and books were shoved inside with no order, no system, just one big mess. His papers, graded and ungraded, were crumpled together, and it always took him at least five minutes to find a pencil. When the teacher collected homework, Tyrone was never quite sure where his homework was. It could be in his desk, or in his bookbag, or maybe folded inside a book. Every time Tyrone had to find something, it was like trying to solve a mystery.

Tyrone felt that it was perfectly normal to be this way, and he didn't see that he had a problem. What was the big deal if he misplaced a paper or two?

But let me tell you that his mother and every teacher he had ever had certainly disagreed with him. They thought it *was* a problem. His mother constantly nagged him. So did all his teachers, and Tyrone wished everyone would just leave him alone. After all, he thought, "We are all different. Not everyone has to do things the same way."

One day, Tyrone's teacher, Mr. Cartwright, called his mom and asked her to come in for a conference. He told Tyrone's mom that he thought Tyrone would do much better in school if he would just organize his things and have a system for doing things.

Tyrone's mom just shook her head. "You know his nickname at home is 'Tyrone the Cyclone.' If you think his desk is bad, you ought to see his room! I would love it if you could come up with a way to get him to clean and organize things. I have nagged him for (AVERAGE AGE OF THE STUDENTS TO WHOM THE STORY IS BEING PRESENTED) years, and that doesn't work at all," she said in a desperate tone of voice.

"Hm–m–m," Mr. Cartwright said, "maybe we should work on a plan together."

And that is what they did!

Tyrone didn't know anything about this conference, and he certainly didn't know that his mom and his teacher were plotting something behind his back. So when he noticed that his teacher's desk was getting rather messy, he didn't suspect a thing! It was funny, though, because the same thing was happening at home. There were pots on the TV, dishes on the couch, and Tyrone thought he saw his mom putting her purse in the oven! Tyrone thought that maybe everyone was starting to see things his way.

One day at school, the class had a huge math assignment: 50 problems! Tyrone worked hard on it and turned it in. When the papers were returned, Tyrone didn't get his back. He went to Mr. Cartwright's desk and asked where his paper was.

"Well, I'm really not sure. I thought it was with the rest of the papers, but maybe it is at home. It could be here somewhere," Mr. Cartwright said, pointing at his desk, which was cluttered with papers, science experiments, and a coffee cup or two. "I really do need that grade, so would you please redo the paper?"

Tyrone was shocked, but what could he say? After all, he had lost a few papers, too. So he sighed and went back to his desk to start doing the assignment again.

Redoing the math assignment was bad enough, but the next day, the same thing happened with a science assignment. Tyrone was losing patience and certainly getting tired of this!

Later that day, during math class, Mr. Cartwright told Tyrone that he had been doing so well in math, he was going to write a "good note" to tell his parents all about it. Tyrone was very happy. His parents liked to hear good news like that.

At the end of the day, Tyrone went to Mr. Cartwright's desk and asked for his note. "Oh, I have been looking for it all afternoon," Mr. Cartwright said. "I don't know what I did with it!"

Tyrone thought for a minute and then politely said, "Well, maybe if we straighten your desk, we can find it."

Mr. Cartwright thought for a moment and said, "Well, I'll tell you what. I'll straighten out my desk right now, if you straighten yours, too."

"Okay," said Tyrone. "It's a deal!"

Tyrone cleaned and organized his desk while his teacher did the same. Mr. Cartwright found the note and the science paper and the original math paper. Tyrone found quite a few interesting things in *his* desk, too, like leftovers from last week's lunch!

When Tyrone took the note home, his parents were thrilled. "Good job," said Dad, giving Tyrone a high-five. "Great!" Mom said. "Why don't we go to Pizza-rama to celebrate?"

Then she started looking all over. "I don't remember what I did with my car keys," she said, as she looked in the pots on the TV set and between the dishes on the couch.

It finally dawned on Tyrone that he had been set up. "I'll tell you what, Mom," Tyrone said, smiling, "I'll help you clean up this mess, if you will help me with my room!"

They both laughed and, at the very same time, Tyrone and his mom said, "It's a deal!"

 Discuss the story by asking the following questions:

"What does *being organized* mean?" *(Accept all appropriate answers and sum up from the answers that being organized is knowing where things are kept, using folders, writing in assignment books, and keeping one's desk clean.)*

"Once you have decided on ways to be organized, how can you be sure your ways will work?" *(To be organized, you must have a system of how to do the things you need to do and stick to that system. For example, if you decide to put your homework in a folder and then put the folder into the bookbag and you always have the bookbag by the door, there is NO WAY you can forget your homework in the morning.)*

Tell the students:

"Research says that if you do something 17 times, it will become habit. You must form organized habits. It may take a few extra seconds to put something in the proper folder or notebook, but it is worth it."

Ask the students:

"How many of you think that you are organized?" *(Count the raised hands.)*

"Those of you who are organized, will you share with the class some organization tricks that you use?" *(Accept all appropriate ideas. You will be surprised by the great ideas students suggest.)*

 Distribute a copy of *Organization Skills* to each student and review each item on the list. Tell the students to keep this paper in a handy place, either at home or school, to remind them of various organizational skills that can be of help to them.

 Activity: Distribute a piece of construction paper and a pencil to each student. Then say:

"Let's get started today. Everyone, organize your desk. Notice that I didn't say *clean out your desk.* I said *organize.* That means there should be a system that you can explain. When you are finished, raise your hand. If you finish before the others, you may use the time to draw. When everyone has finished, I will look in each desk and each student will explain to the class how the desk is organized and what systems *(folders, assignment sheets, bookbags, etc.)* he or she is going to use."

You may want to set a time limit for this activity.

Conclude the lesson by telling the class that you might stage some surprise visits to the classroom for desk inspections and that you expect their desks to always look like they do right now. Tell them to remember that, if they are organized, they won't ever have to clean out their desks again! That's because everything will always be put back in its proper place.

ORGANIZATION SKILLS

✔ Organize your materials at home and at school. This means having a space for everything and putting everything in its space.

✔ Use assignment sheets. Check them before the end of each school day.

✔ Keep a calendar to remind yourself of long-term assignments. Make it a habit to look at the calendar each day!

✔ Set the texts necessary for homework out on the corner of your desk during the school day.

✔ Use a bookbag and have a place at home for it.

✔ Use folders in appropriate ways. Always ask if your teacher requires folders and, if so, how they are to be used.

✔ Make a plan for the next school day at a certain time each evening. This includes planning what you will wear, getting notes and permission slips signed, and packing your bookbag with the things you will need.

LOG
A Lesson on School Success

MATERIALS NEEDED:

- ✔ A list of directions for the students to follow in the listening activity. Make up a list appropriate to the age of the children. The directions should be simple at first and become more complicated as you proceed. Younger children do best with two or three directions, and even fifth-graders cannot remember more than four or five directions. Examples: Stand up, clap your hands once, turn around once, wave at me, sit down. Hop two times on your right foot, pat your head, snap your fingers, and smile!
- ✔ Chalkboard and chalk
- ✔ Copy of *Rap/Rhyme* (page 87), two pieces of construction paper, crayons, paper, and a pencil for each student

LESSON:

The facilitator should:

 Greet the students and ask:

> "How many of you want to get good grades?" *(Hopefully, every student will raise a hand.)*

Then say:

> "That shows a great attitude and, of course, that is always the first step. However, there is more to getting good grades than wishing for them. Some people just don't know the keys that will help them attain success in school. Today I am going to share with you some ideas that could make your wish come true. We are going to begin with a story."

 Read or tell the following story:

> **I want to tell you about a (<u>GRADE LEVEL TO WHICH THE STORY IS BEING PRESENTED</u>) grade girl named Lori. Unfortunately, Lori was not a good student. She didn't like school because she didn't do well, and half the time, she didn't pay attention. To top it off, Lori was very disorganized. Her desk was a mess, she never had the right book at home for her home-**

work, and she often forgot where she put her completed work before it got turned in. You can imagine what Lori's grades were like! Lori had a brother, Brian, who was totally opposite when it came to school. Brian really cared about school and put forth lots of effort. It showed in his grades.

Most of the time, Lori didn't care *what* her grades were. She didn't pay attention to her brother's grades, either, but there were four times a year that she *did* care. These were report-card days. You see, in their family, there was a rule called *"C's or Better."* The rule meant that if you had *C's* or better on your report card, the family had a special night in your honor. You got to pick a restaurant, and the family went out to eat. If you *didn't* get *C's* or better, you didn't even get to go! Well, I guess you know who went and who never got to go.

One report-card night when the family was at Pizza-rama and Lori was sitting in her room all by herself, she started thinking. She thought about her mom and dad and brother out having fun—not to mention pizza—without her. She thought that she really would like to be with them, and that getting good grades would be kind of neat. But she didn't even know where to begin or how to change. She thought and thought, but nothing came to mind. Finally she fell asleep, still thinking about it, but with no answer.

As she slept, Lori had a very strange dream. She dreamt that her teacher, Mrs. Winslow, was there in her bedroom. The difference was that she didn't look like the Mrs. Winslow that Lori knew. She was dressed all in gold. She had wings, and she could fly!

Mrs. Winslow said, "Did I hear you say that you wanted to do better in school? Well, I will share the secret of school success. It is very easy. Just remember LOG!"

"Log? What does a piece of wood have to do with school?" asked Lori.

"No, not log like a piece of wood," said Mrs. Winslow. "LOG like an acronym. L-O-G. If you remember these three rules, your grades will improve. I guarantee it! The *L* stands for *listen during class*. That is the first thing that will help. The *O* stands for *organize*. Get organized at school, at home, and in between. The *G* stands for *goals*. You need to set goals for yourself. Tell yourself that you will do something, and work toward it. That's it! It is as easy as LOG! Just remember LOG! Remember LOG...." And then Mrs. Winslow vanished.

In the morning, when Lori woke, she remembered what happened and thought, "Wow, was that a weird dream!" But then she saw something that made her eyes pop open: There was a sprinkle of gold dust on top of her bookbag!

Lori never did find out whether Mrs. Winslow had actually been in her room that night. She wanted to ask her about it, but she thought it would sound too weird. Instead, she decided to keep the dream to herself. She would remember it, but no one else would ever know about it. She did just that, and the night of the next report–card day, Lori sure did have fun at Taco Palace!

3. Discuss the story by asking the following question:

"What secret to school success did Lori learn about in her dream?" *(She learned the acronym L-O-G. She learned that if she followed it, her grades would improve.)*

Write the letters L-O-G on the chalkboard vertically and have the students explain what the letters stand for. Tell the students that if they remember and try to follow L-O-G, their grades will improve. Then tell the students that although they might later learn other study skills, following the L-O-G rule is a great start.

4. Discuss each letter of L-O-G separately. This discussion could be broken into three separate lessons or completed during one session.

L–LISTENING

Tell the students:

"Many people think that they know how to listen, but listening is not as easy as just being in the same room with someone who is talking. Listening is hard work, and it is the number-one thing that separates good students from poor students. In order for you to listen, your body has to be still, your eyes have to be on the speaker, and your brain has to be thinking about what the speaker is saying. One more hint is that you have to listen to EVERYTHING the person is saying. Does this scenario sound familiar? The teacher tells the students they are going to be doing an art project using crayons. Half of the students dive into their desks, looking for crayons, while the teacher is still explaining the project. In a little while, those same kids are asking what to do. Have you ever done this? Remember, you have to listen to *all* the instructions before you begin any task."

Activity: Tell the students:

"We are going to play a game during which you are to follow the directions I give. Lots of kids say that they cannot remember directions no matter how hard they listen. In order to remember, you have to pretend that you have a miniature tape recorder in your brain. Like a tape recorder, you play back the directions. But unlike a tape recorder, which might keep something forever, you must play it back it right away. This is because research says that the words you hear are there for about seven seconds before they disappear. Therefore, if you can repeat the information immediately, you will be able to remember the directions. The directions I give will be simple at first and then become longer and more complicated. If anyone starts moving in the middle of a list of directions, I will say, 'STOP! Someone is not listening to the WHOLE thing'!" *(Say this with a smile, so no one's feelings will be hurt.)*

Ask the students:

"Are you ready to try? Then let's play a game."

Use the list of directions compiled prior to the lesson. You can follow up this activity with other listening activities. Many enjoyable activities can be found in published material, but it is easy to make up your own.

Distribute crayons and a piece of construction paper to each student. Tell the students to fold the piece of paper in half, in half again, and in half one more time. When the students unfold their papers, each of them will have eight boxes. Show the students how to number their boxes from 1 to 8. Then tell them to draw or write something in each box, using specific colors or directions. For example: Write the word *me* in blue in the middle of box number one. Draw a red circle around the word, and put a yellow square around the whole thing. *(You can change the activities to fit the needs of the children.)*

O–ORGANIZE

Note: If you are presenting this lesson in three separate parts, use *Tyrone the Cyclone* to teach *organization*. If you are presenting this as one lesson and *Tyrone the Cyclone* has already been presented, use this section to review what was learned previously.

Discussion: Ask what *being organized* means. Accept all the students' answers. Sum up from the answers that being organized is knowing where things are kept, using folders and assignment books, and keeping one's desk clean. *(These are typical answers.)* Then say:

"*Being organized* also means having a system of how to do things and not deviating from the system. If you put your homework in a folder and then put the folder into the bookbag and you always leave the bookbag by the door, there is NO WAY you can forget your homework in the morning. Research says that if you do something 17 times, it will become habit. Students must form organized habits. It takes a few extra seconds to put something in the proper folder or notebook, but it is worth it."

Say:

"Raise your hand if you think that you are organized."

Ask those students who raised their hands to share with the class some organization tricks they use. You will be surprised at the great ideas the students suggest!

Appropriate organization skills include:

- organizing your materials at home and school. This means having a space for everything and putting everything in its space.
- using assignment sheets. Check them before the end of each school day.
- keeping a calendar to remind yourself of long-term assignments. Make it a habit to look at the calendar each day!
- setting the texts necessary for homework out on the corner of your desk during the school day.
- using a bookbag and having a place at home for your bookbag.
- using folders in appropriate ways. Always ask if your teacher requires folders and, if so, how they are to be used.
- making a plan for the next school day at a certain time each evening. This includes planning what you will wear, getting notes and permission slips signed, and packing your bookbag with the things you will need.

Activity: The students will want to start getting organized after such a discussion, so say:

"Let's get started today. Everyone, ORGANIZE your desk. Notice that I didn't say *clean out your desk.* There should be a system of organization that you can explain."

Distribute a piece of construction paper, a pencil, and crayons to each student. Tell the students that when they finish organizing their desks, they may draw or write quietly. Tell the students to raise their hands when they have finished organizing their desks. Look in each student's desk and have him/her explain how the desk is organized and what other systems he/she is going to use. *(Folders, assignment sheets, bookbags, etc.)*

Tell the class that you might stage some surprise visits to the classroom for desk inspections and that you expect their desks to always look like they do right now. If they are organized, they won't ever have to clean out their desks, because they will always put everything back in its proper place.

Optional Conclusion: Distribute a copy of *Rap/Rhyme* to each student and say the *Rap/Rhyme* together.

Use the word *organize* frequently in future discussions. Students need to know that becoming organized is a worthy goal for everyone. Do not be afraid to admit if you, the facilitator, are not organized. *(Or good-naturedly tease the classroom teacher if his/her desk is not organized.)* Let the students know that many people strive to become organized.

G–GOAL-SETTING

If you have already taught the lesson *The Bike,* remind the students that in that story Tony got the bike and Sam didn't because Tony set goals. In this story, Lori also had to learn that all successful people set goals for themselves.

If goal-setting has not yet been taught, take enough time to make sure that the students understand the principles behind successful goal-setting:

Activity: Distribute a piece of paper and a pencil to each student. Tell the students:

"Goals must be realistic and measurable. This means that they must be possible for you to achieve and that you must also be able to see whether you were able to meet your goal."

"For example, if you had a *D* in handwriting, you might want to set a goal to improve. To say that you want to do better in handwriting may be realistic, but it is not measurable because it is unclear what *do better* means. How will you know you are doing better?"

"Say you want to improve your handwriting so you can win the school handwriting contest next week. This is a measurable goal because you will know when they announce the winner whether you reached it. But it is not realistic. A student who is currently getting a *D* in handwriting probably cannot improve enough in a week to win a school-wide contest!"

"A goal that is both realistic and measurable would be to improve your handwriting by one letter grade this report-card period. You can try to achieve this goal by turning in all your handwriting work and practicing for 15 minutes three times a week."

"You must also know the difference between long-term goals and short-term goals. A long-term goal might be to know all the multiplication tables through x12 by the end of the school year. To do this, you need to divide your objective into short-term goals. How many tables will you learn in one week? Two weeks? One month? I want you to think about this goal. Imagine that it is four months until the end of the school term and that your goal is to have learned all the multiplication tables by the time you are given a final test. Using your paper and pencil, divide up the time."

Have the students practice dividing long-term goals into short-term goals.

Set a time limit for this activity. When the allotted time has elapsed, allow the students to report what they have done. Write the following example on the chalkboard:

My book report is due within two weeks. My book has 10 chapters, and I haven't started reading it yet. My goal is to turn my book report in on time.

Ask the students:

"Is this goal realistic?" *(Yes, it is realistic because it can be accomplished.)*

"Is this goal measurable?" *(Yes, it is measurable because if the report is turned in by the due date, you can judge whether the goal has been met.)*

"What do you have to do to meet this goal?" *(To meet this goal, the student must break down tasks and make a plan. If the book has 10 chapters and the report is due in two weeks, the student should plan time to read the book and write the report. For example: "I will read two chapters a day and write the report on Sunday, the 12th."*

Write the following example on the chalkboard:

I will get better grades.

Ask the students:

"Is this goal realistic?" *(Yes, the goal is realistic, but it needs to be clarified.)*

"Is this goal measurable?" *(It is not measurable. What does* better grades *mean? How will the students know if they reach this goal?)*

Go to the chalkboard and cross out "I will get better grades." Replace it with: "On my next report card, I will bring my math grade up by one letter grade."

Then ask the students:

"Is the goal realistic and measurable?" *(Yes, it is both realistic and measurable.)*

Have the students break the goal down into short-term goals. When the students have finished, allow them to share their answers with the class.

Next, have each of the students write a goal of his/her own that will ensure school success, then break it down into short-term goals. Also make sure the students pat themselves on the back when they reach their goals!

 Conclude the lesson by reminding the class that, in the story, Lori was able to improve her grades by using the L-O-G principles. Challenge the students and tell them that if they try implementing these three simple techniques, you guarantee that their grades will improve!

RAP

Do yourself a favor and organize.
It'll help a lot more than you realize.

Have a system, a plan, or otherwise,
You'll waste a lot of time when you apologize.

Use dividers and folders you can alphabetize.
A planner is great, because it simplifies.

With your papers, find ways to categorize.
Then you won't lose things and be mortified.

So do yourself a favor and get organized.
Then you'll find success and be recognized!

RHYME

*Organize, organize. **
Please don't be a mess! **
Organize, organize,
Always straighten your desk.
Organize, organize.
You will do your best!
Organize, organize.
And you'll always pass the test.
Organize, organize.
You be a big success.
Organize, organize.
Each and every day!

---

* Have the students say the part in italics.
** The facilitator says this part. Feel free to add to it. The sillier, the better!

SCHOOL COOL
A Lesson about Responsibility in Learning

Note: This is a good lesson to use as the culmination of a unit on study skills.

MATERIALS NEEDED:

✔ Copy of *Am I School Cool?* (page 93), *I Am School Cool* (page 94), paper, a pencil, and crayons or markers for each student
✔ List of responsible and irresponsible behaviors (optional). Some examples are:

- LaToya uses the dictionary to look up words that she doesn't know how to spell.
- Joey reads a book quietly when he is finished with his work.
- Lanie runs down the hall when no one is looking.
- Harold starts his book report the night before it is due.
- The night before a big test, Kayla stays up until midnight studying.
- Tim writes assignments in a planner and takes home all the books he needs.

LESSON:

The facilitator should:

 Tell the students:

"In other lessons, we have discussed many things that will help you improve your grades and become a better student. But of all the topics we have talked about, today's lesson may be the most important. Let me start with a story."

 Read or tell the following story:

At Wendell School, there were many after-school clubs. There were clubs for kids interested in photography, drama, computers, sports, math, and many other things. But the club everyone wanted to join was the "School Cool" Club.

The reason that everyone wanted to be in the "School Cool" Club is because the teacher, who is the club sponsor, always plans fabulous events. One time, she planned a cave-exploration field trip. All of the club members went to Dinmar Cave on a Saturday. They explored the cave and had a picnic afterward. Another time, the club was invited to the University's Science Lab. College students worked with the club members and they conducted scientific experiments all day. Everybody at school heard about these events and wanted to be a part of them.

But nobody was quite sure what to do to get invited to be in the club. It was different from all the rest of the clubs at Wendell. With all the other clubs, all you had to do to join was sign up. But you had to be *invited* to join the "School Cool" Club. Everyone knew that this club was only for students who were responsible, good citizens at Wendell and who took their education seriously. Somehow, in your classroom, you had to prove to your teacher that you were "School Cool," and usually only one kid from each classroom was asked to join the club. Being "School Cool" didn't mean that you had to get straight *A's*. Some of the members of the club got B's, and some even had *C's* on their report cards. But somehow, you had to prove that you were "School Cool."

Sara Phillips, in (<u>GRADE LEVEL TO WHICH THE STORY IS BEING PRESENTED</u>) grade, was no different than anyone else at Wendell. She really wanted to be asked to join the "School Cool" Club, but she just didn't know what to do.

One day, Sara's teacher, Mrs. Parks, announced a contest for her (<u>GRADE LEVEL TO WHICH THE STORY IS BEING PRESENTED</u>) grade classroom. She said that if all the students completed all of their homework for a month, the class could have a special free day. There would be no work or lessons on that day and everyone could bring games and crafts to share. Everyone would be free for the whole day to choose activities and have fun.

Sara and everyone else in the class thought this sounded like a dream come true. They decided right then and there that they could accomplish what Mrs. Parks wanted if they worked together. It was a great month! Everyone helped everyone else by giving compliments and words of encouragement. The students developed a phone chain to remind one another about assignments and offered help to anyone having trouble completing the work.

When the end of the month came, Mrs. Parks announced that the class had achieved its goal. Every single student had completed all the work for a whole month. The class cheered when Mrs. Parks kept her word and said that Monday would be "Free Choice Day."

Sunday night, Sara was so excited that she could hardly sleep. She planned to take her rug-hooking project to school, and she knew that two of her best friends were taking games she loved to play.

Monday morning, Mrs. Parks said that the students had complete freedom to do whatever they wanted as long as they didn't disturb other classes.

Sara couldn't wait to start her rug. As she began to get her supplies together, she glanced at the clock and noticed that it was the time the class usually copied the weekly spelling words. Then a sudden thought struck her. How would she get a good grade on the test on Friday if she hadn't copied the words? She decided that she would first copy the words, then begin her rug. She wrote each word carefully and checked to make sure that she had spelled it correctly. Then, as she was about to start hooking her rug, she remembered the book her class had been reading on Friday. They had stopped at a very exciting place, and she wondered what was going to happen to the main character. Sara went up to Mrs. Parks' desk and asked, "Would you mind if I read a little from our book?"

Mrs. Parks said, "No, Sara. After all, it *is* "Free Choice Day."

Sara read for a good part of the morning.

After lunch, Mrs. Parks told everyone to continue with "Free Choice Day." Sara was planning to join her friends, who were about to begin playing a board game, when she noticed that Mrs. Parks was sitting up at her desk watching the students enjoy themselves. Sara thought that since Mrs. Parks was not too busy, this would be a great chance to get some help on the division problems the class had been working on lately. She went and asked for some individual help. Then, when she thought she understood how to do the problems, Sara went back to her desk and did some practice problems. When she was finished, she went up to the teacher's desk and asked her to grade them to see if she had done them correctly. After Mrs. Parks checked the problems, she smiled and said that Sara seemed to understand how to do them.

Sara looked at the clock and noticed that "Free Choice Day" was almost over. She really didn't have enough time now to work on her rug and her friends were in the middle of a game, so Sara thought she would spend some time organizing her desk and checking her assignment book for the next day. Then she decided to use the remaining time to study for the next week's social studies test.

Just as the bell was about to ring, Mrs. Parks called Sara up to her desk and said, "Sara, I've been watching you today. Even though it was 'Free Choice Day,' you spent your time doing spelling, reading, math, and social studies."

Sara said, "Yes, ma'am, I suppose that I did."

Mrs. Parks said, "Well, that proves to me that you care enough about your education to work even when nobody makes you do it. That shows a lot of responsibility, and that is very 'School Cool.' Welcome to the club!"

At first, Sara could not believe what she was hearing. But when she realized it was true, all she could do was reply with a huge "School Cool" smile!

 Discuss the story by asking the students the following question:

"Why do you think Sara was asked to join the club?" *(She took responsibility for her education on her own without being told to do so.)*

Spend time making the point that students who are responsible for themselves and their learning are very "School Cool." These students realize that education is not a plot to keep them busy, but a program to benefit them and enrich their lives.

Activity: Divide the class into small groups *(or leave the class as a large group)*. Distribute a piece of paper and a pencil to each small group or to each student. Tell the students to brainstorm about ways that students prove they are responsible or "School Cool." Have them write their answers on the paper. Set a time limit for the activity.

When the allotted time has elapsed, have the students share their answers. If not included in the students' presentations, add the following to the list:

- complete work with no reminding or nagging from teachers or parents
- desire to keep desk and supplies organized and neat and do so
- use time wisely at school because they want to do their best
- follow school and classroom rules because doing so will help them learn
- put forth their best effort because they want to get the most out of their education
- make every effort to get along with others and to consider the feelings of classmates
- use an organized system of keeping up with assignments (folders, planners, calendars, etc.) because they want to succeed
- do above and beyond what is required.

The above activity can be changed into a game if the facilitator uses a prepared list of "School Cool" behaviors and irresponsible school behaviors. Mix the two lists together. As each behavior is read, the students determine if it is irresponsible or "School Cool." If the behavior is responsible, the students should say "School Cool" aloud. Students have fun trying to say this in a "cool" way.

The game should be played only long enough for students to pick up on the differences between irresponsible and responsible behaviors.

5 Tell the students:

"It's obvious to me that you can recognize "School Cool" behavior in other people. I wonder if you can recognize it in yourself."

Distribute a copy of *Am I School Cool?* and a pencil to each student. Instruct the students to be honest, because dishonesty only results in them fooling themselves. Explain that no one will see their sheets unless they choose to share them. Tell them that there are no certain numbers that tell if they are "School Cool," but that 4's and 3's are preferred. Any 2's or 1's can be improved upon by setting goals. When the students finish the sheet, have them turn the paper over and write goals for strengthening their weak areas.

6 Conclude the lesson by distributing the *I Am School Cool* poster and crayons. When the students have finished coloring the poster, tell them they may take both activity sheets home.

AM I SCHOOL COOL?

**Answer these questions about yourself.
Use these numbers:**

Always = 4   Usually = 3   Sometimes = 2   Hardly ever = 1

_____ 1. I get myself up in the morning.

_____ 2. I get dressed for school in plenty of time.

_____ 3. I brush my teeth and hair before I leave the house.

_____ 4. I remember my books, lunch, and materials.

_____ 5. I get to my classroom on time.

_____ 6. I keep my desk organized.

_____ 7. I remember my homework and turn it in on time.

_____ 8. I complete all my assignments.

_____ 9. I do not disturb others during work time.

_____ 10. I am quiet and do not run in the hall.

_____ 11. I remember my lunch or my lunch money.

_____ 12. I write down assignments and remember my books.

_____ 13. I put my bookbag in the same place every night.

_____ 14. I do my homework without being told.

_____ 15. I do my chores at home without being told.

_____ 16. I go to bed at my bedtime without being told.

_____ 17. I do my work even when I'm not "in the mood."

_____ 18. I follow school and classroom rules.

_____ 19. I listen in class.

_____ 20. I do my best in school.

_____ 4's   _____ 3's   _____ 2's   _____ 1's

I AM SCHOOL COOL

OR AT LEAST I'M WORKING ON IT!

TAMARA'S WISH
A Lesson on Test–Taking

MATERIALS NEEDED:

✔ Puppet
✔ Paper and pencil for each student group
✔ Chalkboard and chalk
✔ Copy of *Practice Test* (pages 100-101) and pencil for each student

LESSON:

The facilitator should:

 Introduce the puppet by name. Then have the following conversation with the puppet:

Facilitator:	"Hi, (<u>NAME OF PUPPET</u>), how are you doing?"
Puppet:	"Well, I'm a little worried. I have a big test tomorrow, and I hate tests."
Facilitator:	"I know some people really hate tests, but there are others who *like* taking tests because that's a time to show off what they have learned. *(Speak to the class)* Boys and girls, raise your hands if you hate tests. Now, boys and girls, raise your hands if you *don't* hate tests. *(Turn back to the puppet)* I know of a girl who didn't like to take tests because she was afraid of them. But believe it or not, she learned to *like* them. Let me tell you her story."

2 Read or tell the following story:

Once upon a time, there was a (<u>GRADE LEVEL TO WHICH THE STORY IS BEING PRESENTED</u>) grade girl named Tamara who was afraid of taking tests.

Tamara usually scored *A's* or *B's* on her daily assignments, but when her teacher put the same questions on paper and called it a test, Tamara's mind would freeze and she would forget everything she knew.

Tests scared Tamara. In fact, tests *terrified* her! Whenever there was going to be a test, Tamara's heart would beat fast, her palms would get sweaty, and she would start thinking all kinds of negative thoughts. She *knew* that she was going to do poorly, and you know what? She

---

usually did. She would always get herself upset and nervous before a test and usually would not be able to calm down until it was all over. Tamara really dreaded taking tests!

One day, Tamara's class started a unit on fairy tales. The teacher told the students that they were to select their favorite fairy tale and then report to the class why they liked it. This was going to be easy for Tamara. Her favorite fairy tale had always been—and always would be—*Cinderella.* She liked the story because Cinderella had something Tamara wished *she* had: a great fairy godmother.

Later that same day, Tamara's teacher announced that the class would be taking standardized achievement tests the following week. When Tamara heard this, she instantly broke into a sweat. "Oh, no, I am going to flunk!" she thought.

That night, Tamara couldn't sleep. All she could think about were those tests. She recalled the Cinderella story and thought, "Boy, could I use a fairy godmother now!"

All of a sudden, Tamara saw a flash of light and a beautiful lady dressed in gold and silver appeared at the end of the bed. She looked kind of like the good witch in *The Wizard of Oz.*

"Hello, Tamara. Do you need help?" the beautiful lady asked.

"Who are you?" asked Tamara.

"I'm the person you wished for. I'm your fairy godmother!"

"You can't be. Fairy godmothers are only in fairy tales. If you're really my fairy godmother, how come I haven't seen you before?" Tamara asked.

"You never called for me before," the beautiful lady said. "But now that you have and now that I am here, you have your one chance. How can I help?"

Tamara said, "Well, if you really are my fairy godmother, I need some magic to help me do well next week on our standardized achievement tests. I am really scared of tests, and I never do well."

"You don't need magic to do well on tests" her fairy godmother said. "You just need to learn some test-taking tips. I'll give you a few pointers and you'll do fine!"

The beautiful lady sat down with Tamara and told her some test-taking tips. Then she even had Tamara sit down and take a practice test. Tamara did pretty well on the practice test and even relaxed a little.

Before the fairy godmother disappeared, she asked Tamara, "Is there anything else? Now is your chance!"

Tamara said, "No, you've done a lot for me! Thank you."

With a flash of her silver- and gold-gown, the beautiful lady disappeared.

The next week, Tamara's class was given the test. Tamara took a deep breath and followed many of the tips that her fairy godmother had taught her. She wasn't nervous at all, and she did fine on the test.

Tamara was very happy, until about two days after the test. That's when she realized that she had missed a great opportunity. She had had her fairy godmother with her. She could have wished for anything in the world, and all she asked for was help on tests. She should have asked for a pony!

Tamara tried and tried to get her fairy godmother back. But no matter what she did, her fairy godmother did not appear. Tamara never saw her again. Tamara never did get her pony. But she sure didn't worry about taking tests anymore!

 Tell the students that today you are going to be each one's fairy godmother/father and that you will help them learn to feel more comfortable about taking tests.

Ask the students:

"Why do many schools have students take standardized tests?" (Giving standardized tests is the schools' way of seeing what their students know in comparison with other students in the same grade around the country. Standardized tests also help teachers measure what their students have learned and what they still need to teach them. [This explanation often helps relieve some of students' anxieties.])

Tell the students:

"Almost no one is able to correctly answer every question on a standardized test. That's because some of the questions might be about something that a middle-school or high-school student might know. These questions are included in the test just to find out how much knowledge a student may have. Sometimes students don't do well on tests because they ignore or haven't heard of some simple tips that can make test-taking easier. You may or may not know quite a few hints already. So in order for me to find out what you know, I am dividing the class into several small groups. Each group will have the same topic: What can students do *before* a test to improve their scores? Select one person to be the leader of the group, one to be the recorder, and one person to be the reporter. The reporter in your group will report your ideas to the class."

Divide the students into groups. Distribute a piece of paper and a pencil to each group. Set a time limit for this activity.

When the allotted time has elapsed, ask each group to report its findings. Record the information on the chalkboard. *(If class time is limited, you can provide the information instead of doing groupwork or discuss the question as a large group and elicit answers.)* If the groups' answers do not include the following, add them to the list written on the chalkboard.

- Have a good attitude: "I can do it."
- Be prepared. Have the necessary supplies, sharpened pencils, etc.
- Get a good night's sleep.
- Eat a healthy breakfast.
- Use nervousness to improve performance. (Emphasize that *everyone*, including famous athletes and actors, gets nervous before a performance. Explain that people can turn nervousness into energy by taking deep breaths and visualizing their success.)
- Study. (This doesn't always apply to a standardized achievement test, but it can't hurt!)

After the groups have reported their findings, continue the discussion by asking the following questions:

"What can students do *during* a test that will help bring success?" *(They can:*

- *work steadily, especially if the test is timed.*
- *read all directions and questions carefully.*
- *guess, if they don't know an answer. [On many standardized tests, they will not be penalized for guessing incorrectly.]*
- *put forth continuous effort.*
- *stay in their seats and be quiet.)*

"What are some tips for using an answer sheet that will be scored by a machine or computer?" *(Test-takers should:*

- *always be sure to be on the right problem. [Compare the number of the question to the number on the answer sheet for each question.]*
- *make no stray marks on the answer sheet. [Tests are scored by machines that can't tell a stray mark from an answer.]*
- *use a #2 pencil.*
- *fill in each answer space completely.*
- *keep the answer sheet unwrinkled and clean.)*

"What are some tips on answering multiple-choice questions?" *(Test-takers should:*

- *read all the choices before selecting an answer.*
- *eliminate answers that are obviously wrong.*
- *narrow down the answers to two possible choices and guess if unsure.*
- *remember that correct answers very seldom have absolutes. If an answer uses words like* always *or* never*, it is probably wrong. This is also a good tip for True/False questions.)*

 Distribute a copy of the *Practice Test* and a pencil to each student. Have the students complete the test. Set a time limit for this activity. If desired, students may correct their own papers. Discuss why each answer is correct. The *Practice Test* answers are:

1. c. nicotine
2. d. having a heart attack
3. b. "The Effects of Nicotine on the Body"
4. b. has seen
5. d. Correct as it is
6. b. amazing
7. d. No mistake
8. d. 375
9. e. NH
10. b. $5.50

 Conclude the session by using the puppet to lead the following cheer:

Take a test!
Do your best!
Show 'em what you know!

Don't despair!
Just take care
To let your learning show!

When finished, ask the puppet:

Facilitator: "Well, (NAME OF PUPPET), how to you feel about taking tests now?"
Puppet: "Pretty good. I'm not as worried as I was before. In fact, I'm kind of looking forward to using the new things I've learned in tomorrow's test."

PRACTICE TEST

Directions: On this section of the test, you must read the paragraph and read the questions below it. Read the questions carefully and choose the best answer. Questions #1-#3 go with the paragraph.

When people smoke cigarettes, they inhale a powerful drug called *nicotine* into their bodies. Nicotine makes the heart beat faster. The blood vessels narrow, making it harder for the blood to flow through them. This means the heart has to work harder to bring oxygen to the body.

1.   The drug in cigarettes is called _____ .
     a.   caffeine
     b.   cocaine
     c.   nicotine
     d.   tobacco

2.   After reading this paragraph, a person might guess that a smoker has the possible risk of _____ .
     a.   developing cancer
     b.   getting out of breath
     c.   having bad breath
     d.   having a heart attack

3.   The best name for this paragraph would be _____ .
     a.   "Smoking is Bad for You"
     b.   "The Effects of Nicotine on the Body"
     c.   "Second-Hand Smoke"
     d.   "Just Say No"

LANGUAGE:

Read each sentence and look at the bold underlined word or phrase. Ask yourself if the word or phrase is correct as it is or if it needs to be changed. Choose the answer that makes the sentence correct.

4.   Wendy **seen** that movie two times already!
     a.   have seen
     b.   has seen
     c.   will see
     d.   Correct as it is

---

5.   The **delicious dinner was served** at 6:00.
        a.   The delicious dinner, was served at 6:00.
        b.   The delicious, dinner was served at 6:00
        c.   The delicious dinner, it was served at 6:00.
        d.   Correct as it is

SPELLING:

Read each sentence below and notice the bold underlined word. Are any of the words incorrect, or are there no mistakes in any of the sentences? Choose the sentence with the misspelled word. If there are no misspelled words, choose the last answer: "No Mistake."

6.   a.   Sandy was the **second** one to finish.
     b.   That is an **amasing** story.
     c.   He knew the right **answer**.
     d.   No mistake

7.   a.   You will have to wait a **minute**.
     b.   His piece of cake was **equal** in size to mine.
     c.   Sandy received extra **credit** on her project.
     d.   No mistake

MATH:

Work these problems on a piece of scratch paper. Choose the correct answer. If the correct answer does not appear, choose NH, which stands for "Not Here."

8.   345 + 30 =
     a. 365   b. 395   c. 360   d. 375   e. NH

9.   400 - 150 =
     a. 200   b. 150   c. 350   d. 300   e. NH

10. Julie sold hot dogs at the school carnival. They cost $1.50 apiece. If Bob bought three hot dogs and gave Julie $10.00, how much should she give him in change?

     a. $4.50   b. $5.50   c. $4.00   d. $ 6.25   e. NH

DEAN DECIDES
A Lesson on Decision–Making

MATERIALS NEEDED:

✔ Copy of *Decision-Making Situations* (pages 108-109) and pencil for each group (or student)
✔ Chalkboard and chalk

LESSON:

The facilitator should:

 Introduce the lesson by saying:

"Today's lesson concerns one of the most important topics that I know of. It's about something you do every day. Can anyone tell me what it might be?" *(Have the students guess different topics. If someone guesses "decision-making," announce that that answer is correct, but that decision-making is only a part of the answer. If no one guesses the correct answer within a reasonable period of time, tell the students the answer. Continue with the remarks below:)*

"Yes, today's lesson is about making decisions. But we all know that there are two kinds of decisions that can be made. Can anyone tell me what the two kinds of decisions are?" *(Have the students answer "Good" and "Bad.")*

"Again, you are right. Now if we put the two answers together, what do you think the important topic for today is?" *(Elicit the answer "making good or positive decisions.")*

Then say:

"Some of you don't look too thrilled, so let me begin the lesson with a story about a boy who didn't think this sounded like a very interesting subject."

 Read or tell the following story:

Dean is a boy who doesn't like school. In fact, he thinks school is a major waste of time. Every time his teacher says, "Get out your spelling book," (or English book or reading book or social studies book) Dean rolls his eyes and thinks "Oh, great! We are going to learn something stupid that I will never use in the real world! Am I ever going to need to know what a *pronoun* is when I am finished with school? Why should

I learn spelling when I have a spell-check on my computer? And who cares what *longitude* and *latitude* are or what the definition of *plateau* is?"

Everyone who sees Dean knows exactly how he feels. He doesn't try to hide it. Along with the rolling eyes, he sighs heavily, shakes his head, slouches in his chair, and certainly doesn't rush to take out whatever book the teacher has asked for.

What makes the problem worse is that Dean is a leader in his class. A lot of the other kids admire him and try to act just like him.

One Friday, the school counselor, Mr. Brown, came into the classroom to present a lesson. He said, "Class, today we will be talking about the steps involved in making good decisions."

Before he could say anything more, Dean went into his "attitude" pose. Immediately, several other students assumed the same position. Mr. Brown noticed it right away. "Dean, do you have a problem today?" he asked.

"No," Dean muttered unconvincingly.

Mr. Brown said, "You know that I always encourage all of you to express your feelings. And since I can see that something is wrong, I would like you to tell me what it is."

"Well, Mr. Brown, no offense, but I think this is a major waste of time. Why would we want to learn about decision-making?"

"Yeah," agreed the group of kids who imitated Dean's behavior.

Mr. Brown smiled and said, "I don't want to waste my time or yours. I'll tell you what. I won't teach the lesson today. I want you to think about the topic over the weekend. I will come back on Monday. If you really think it is a waste of time, I won't teach the lesson at all. But at least give me the courtesy of really thinking about why it might be important to learn about making decisions."

"Okay," said Dean, "it's a deal."

Of course, Dean really had no intention of giving the matter any thought at all. He decided he would just tell Mr. Brown that he didn't need to learn about decisions and that would be that. Dean really felt good. He liked having the power to determine what Mr. Brown would teach.

When Dean got home from school that afternoon, his mom greeted him at the door. "Dean, since your dad is out of town on a business trip, I thought you and I would just go out to eat and then rent a movie to watch on the VCR," she said. "Where do you want to go to eat?"

Dean was just about to tell her, when he had a thought. "Hey, Mom, that's a decision!"

She looked at him strangely and said, "Yes, it is. Now what have you decided?"

Dean chose a Mexican restaurant. After he and his mom got there, he had to decide what to eat. Dean couldn't get over that he'd had to make two decisions in the few hours since school had ended for the day.

After dinner, they went to the video store. "What do you want to see?" Mom asked.

"Mom, do you know you are asking me to make another decision?" asked Dean.

Again, she looked at him and said, "Yes. So?"

"Well, that's three in the last hour."

"Okay," Dean's mom answered. "And here's another one. Tomorrow we are going to visit Grandma. Do you want to go before or after lunch?"

Dean just stared at his mom, surprised at the number of decisions he had had to make in such a short time.

On Saturday, after Dean and his mom had visited Grandma, his best friend, Glenn, came over to the house. "Hey, Dean," he asked, "want to go skate boarding for a while this afternoon or would you rather join the rest of the guys playing football in the park?"

Dean couldn't get over the fact that he had another decision to make. It seemed that everywhere he went, he had to make decisions.

During the rest of the weekend, Dean counted 248 decisions he had to make. Some were small matters, but a couple of them were important to him, like:

• Should he spend his birthday money on a video game or save it for the new bike he wanted?

- Should he help his little brother with his homework or do his own?
- Should he take the shortcut down the alley or walk home along the well-lit sidewalk?
- Should he listen to his mom or to his friends?

By Monday, Dean realized that life was a long string of decisions. Making decisions, right or wrong, could change his life.

Mr. Brown, the counselor, walked into the classroom at 2:00. Dean was sitting upright in his chair, eager to learn. Mr. Brown looked at Dean and said, "Well, what's your decision? Is this an important topic or not?" Dean looked at him and answered, "Since I had to make 248 decisions this weekend and some of them were very important, I guess you were right. So, Mr. Brown, will you teach us to make good decisions?"

The rest of the class looked at Dean and followed his lead. They sat up straight and said, "Yeah!"

3. Look at the class, smile, and say:

"Now let's see that same attitude in here!" *(Wait until everyone sits up straight and smiles!)*

Tell the students:

"When you were a baby, you didn't have to make any decisions. Your parents made every decision for you. But little by little, parents start turning that responsibility over to their children as they grow up and as they seem ready to make good choices. The older you get, the more decisions you will be making."

Ask the following questions:

"What decisions have you made already today?" *(Let them name a few. They will probably name small matters, such as what to wear, what to eat for breakfast, etc.)*

"Many of the decisions you make every day are small, but some can be major. Can you think of any decisions that you might make that could change your life?" *(Whether to do something dangerous, whether to work hard in school, whether to take a sip or two of alcohol or smoke a cigarette, etc.)*

"What is a *consequence*?" *(A consequence is something that occurs as a result of a decision.)*

"How do you think that anyone is able to tell whether he or she is making a good, positive decision?" *(All decisions have consequences—positive or negative—and by thinking the consequences through, anyone can tell whether the decision made is most likely to be positive or negative.)*

"If someone decided to complete his homework every night, would the consequences probably be positive or negative?" *(Positive)*

"Kids often take up bad habits, such as smoking, because many consequences don't occur immediately. For example, if someone decided to skip brushing his or her teeth, what might happen?" *(His/her teeth would get cavities and maybe even have to be pulled.)* "Would deciding not to brush your teeth be a negative decision or a positive decision?" *(Negative)* "When would the consequences occur?" *(After you hadn't brushed your teeth for a while.)*

"What does a person have to do to make good, positive decisions?" *(Predict what the consequences will be BEFORE the decision is made. However, some consequences are not easy to predict!)*

 Tell the students that the steps to making a good decision are D.B.C.C. Then write the following steps to making a good decision on the chalkboard.

D - Decision to make?
B - Brainstorm your alternatives.
C - Consider the consequences.
C - Choose the best alternative.

Teach the students the following rhyme:

D.B.C.C.
The steps are easy, don't you agree?
When you have to decide or make a choice,
Just use your brain before your voice!
The steps are easy, don't you agree?
D.B.C.C.

 Say to the students:

"Let's try using D.B.C.C. and think out loud together. The situation is this: Judi breaks a glass in the kitchen. The first step is D. Is there a decision to make?" *(She has to decide what she should do.)* "The second step is B. What are some alternatives she could brainstorm?" *(She could clean up the broken glass herself and not tell her mom; she could call her mom into the kitchen to clean up the mess; she could leave the broken glass on the floor; she could call her mom into the kitchen, apologize, and offer to help clean up the glass.)* "The third step is C. What are the probable consequences of each brainstorm possibility?" *(If Judi cleans up the broken glass by herself:*

- she could cut herself.
- she could do a wonderful job and everything would be fine.
- she could leave a piece of glass on the floor and her mom might later cut her foot.
- her mom could look for the glass and ask where it is. When Judi tells her, it might appear that she had been sneaky about the accident.
- her mom might be angry at her for breaking the glass.

If Judi calls her mom to clean up the mess:

- her mom might say she is lazy.
- her mom might think she is not responsible.

If Judi leaves the broken glass on the floor:

- the next person to come into the room might get cut.

If Judi calls her mom in, apologizes, and offers to help clean up the glass:

- her mom will think she is a responsible person.
- her mom will know it was an accident.
- her mom will help get all the glass off the floor.
- her mom might get angry.)

"The fourth step is C. After reviewing all of the probable consequences, what is the best choice?" *(The best choice is for Judi to call her mom in, apologize, and offer to help clean up the glass.)*

 Divide the students into groups. Distribute a copy of *Decision-Making Situations* and a pencil to each group. Have the students discuss the situations and practice making positive decisions by using the D.B.C.C. steps. *(Or choose one situation and have each student practice the D.B.C.C. steps independently.)* Set a time limit for this activity. When the allotted time has elapsed, discuss each group's decisions.

 Conclude the lesson by having the students recite this rhyme:

D.B.C.C.
The steps are easy, don't you agree?
When you have to decide or make a choice,
Just use your brain before your voice!
The steps are easy, don't you agree?
D.B.C.C.

DECISION-MAKING SITUATIONS

Read each situation. Using D.B.C.C., make a decision about the situation.

1. Kerry has a big report due on Tuesday. It is Monday night, and he always has soccer practice on Monday night.

   D. _____
   B. _____
   C. _____
   C. _____

2. Danielle just moved into a new neighborhood. She can invite only one person over to her house on the weekend. She doesn't know whether to invite her old friend from her old neighborhood or a new friend she just met.

   D. _____
   B. _____
   C. _____
   C. _____

3. Jim has to decide what is the best way to study for his social studies test. Some of Jim's friends want him to study with them, but he also learns when he studies by himself.

   D. _____
   B. _____
   C. _____
   C. _____

4. Janet has been saving her money for a new bike. She has $20.00 so far. Now some of her friends want her to go bowling with them. That will cost $8.00.

D. _____

B. _____

C. _____

C. _____

5. Charles is excited about a big field trip his class is taking. On the day of the field trip, he wakes up feeling sick.

D. _____

B. _____

C. _____

C. _____

6. Terrill is afraid of storms. He is invited to a sleepover on Friday. The weatherman has predicted thunderstorms for that night.

D. _____

B. _____

C. _____

C. _____

7. Anthony has to do his homework every night. He gets to choose when to do it.

D. _____

B. _____

C. _____

C. _____

8. Vivian gets to choose what kind of pet the family will get.

D. _____

B. _____

C. _____

C. _____

THE PARK STREET 10
A Lesson on Peer Pressure

Note: Use this lesson as a follow-up lesson to *Dean Decides.*

MATERIALS NEEDED:

✔ Four notecards (eight, if dealing with a large class)

LESSON:

The facilitator should:

 Greet the students and remind them that, in a previous lesson, they learned the steps to making good decisions. Ask the students:

> "Do you remember the rhyme about the decision-making steps?" *(If the answer is "Yes," recite the rhyme together. If the students need a review of what the rhyme was, recite the rhyme below for the class. Then recite the rhyme with the class.)*

> D.B.C.C.
> The steps are easy, don't you agree?
> When you have to decide or make a choice,
> Just use your brain before your voice!
> The steps are easy, don't you agree?
> D.B.C.C.

Review the following D.B.C.C. steps with the class:

> **D** - Decision to make?
> **B** - Brainstorm your alternatives.
> **C** - Consider the consequences.
> **C** - Choose the best alternative.

Say to the students:

> "I know this sounds pretty easy, but certain things can make it a little more complicated. One complication is when your friends are involved. Let me tell you a story about a girl who had to make a decision."

2 Read or tell the following story:

(<u>AGE TO WHICH THE STORY IS BEING PRESENTED</u>) year-old Chris Simmons thought that she lived in the best neighborhood in the world. What made it so great was the fact that lots of kids around her age lived there, too. On her block, Chris was one of about 10 kids who had grown up together. They had been friends since kindergarten and played together whenever they had the chance. When the children were in third grade, one of their parents referred to them as the "Park Street 10," and somehow that name had stuck.

The "Park Street 10" played and enjoyed being outside in every season. Fall was great because the air was crisp and cool and they romped in the leaves, trick-or-treated together, and organized events like hayrides and apple-bobbing contests. In the winter, they sledded and built snowmen and had some great snowball fights. Of course, spring was a nice time because, as the weather warmed up, they were all out in the evenings, enjoying the freedom of riding bikes, playing ball and other games, and not wearing coats.

But of all the seasons, the "Park Street 10's" favorite was summer. There was no school, and they were free to play and have fun every single day.

The only problem was that sometimes they had a hard time deciding what to do. With a group that large, there were bound to be some disagreements. One person might say, "Let's go swimming." Another would say, "No, let's go to the park!" This led to arguments, and the kids usually spent at least an hour arguing about which activity would be more fun.

Last summer, during one of those disagreements, Chris came up with a great idea. She suggested that they take turns deciding where the group would play. "Let's make an agreement right now," she said. "Each day, one person will set the schedule for the day and everyone else will participate in those plans. Each one of us will get a turn to choose what to do, so it will be fair. We can go in alphabetical order." Everyone liked the idea and agreed that one person would pick the event each day. After that, there were no more arguments.

Abby's turn came first, and she chose swimming. Everyone loved to swim, and they all enjoyed splashing and racing through the blue water of the community pool.

The day Chris got to choose, there was a carnival in town. Going to the carnival is what she chose to do. They all had a great time riding the rides and trying their luck at the booths.

When it was Joe's day to choose, he had the friends hike on the trail that wound through the woods behind their neighborhood.

Nick chose staying around his house and playing old favorites, such as Hide and Seek, Freeze Tag, and Tetherball.

The day Richard got to choose, he said, "Today, let's ride our bikes down to the railroad tracks. One of my cousins told me that you can find neat stuff down there." They all got on their bikes and they were ready to go when Chris spoke up.

"I don't think we should do that," she said.

"Why not?" asked Richard.

"It doesn't sound safe to me," Chris replied.

"We aren't going to ride *on* the tracks," said Richard. "We'll keep back a few feet."

"No, I'm not going," said Chris.

Everyone stopped and stared at Chris. Joel spoke up first. "Chris, you are the one who came up with the plan to take turns picking the activity. We all did what *you* wanted to do when it was your turn. It's not fair for you to back out when it is Richard's turn."

"Yeah," said Richard. "I went to your thing. Now you have to go along with my idea."

"I'm sorry, but I don't think it sounds safe and I am not going to go. I don't think you guys should go, either!" said Chris.

Richard was very upset that Chris was being so stubborn. "Come on," he said. "We don't need her. In fact, I think the 'Park Street 9' sounds pretty good. Chris, if you think you can boss us around, you can forget about being part of the group."

Chris said, "I don't want to lose your friendship, but I can't do something that I don't think is right. I'm going to the park."

As Chris rode off, she was sure she had lost her friends. She felt horrible and sick to her stomach. She cried as she rode, and she didn't know what she was going to do by herself for the rest of the summer. She had almost reached the park when she heard someone shouting.

Abby rode up, puffing. "Wow!" she exclaimed. "I didn't think I was going to be able to catch up with you. I wanted to say that I think you are right. It's not safe to go to the tracks. Even though we have always stuck together, we do have our own minds and we have to use them. It was so brave of you to stand up to everyone and tell them how you feel."

Chris smiled through her tears and said, "Thanks, Abby. At least we will have each other."

Just then, they turned and saw the rest of the kids. Richard was looking kind of embarrassed when he said, "Chris, I started using my brain, too. I guess the railroad tracks isn't the best place to play. It's my day to choose, and I think we should spend the day at the park, having races. Last one to the slide is a rotten egg!"

The "Park Street 10" had a great day that day. And after that, they agreed that it is okay to disagree!

 Discuss the story by asking the following question and introducing the activities.

"Why was the decision Chris made so difficult?" *(Not only did she have to use the D.B.C.C. steps for herself, she had to stand up to her friends and say "No.")*

Say to the students:

"There is a name for something that often interferes with a person calmly going through the decision-making steps. See if you can guess what it is. We will play a game like *Wheel of Fortune.* I will call on one student to give me a letter. If the letter is correct, the class will receive a point. If the letter is not found in the word, the class will lose a point. When you discover the word, you will know the topic for today's lesson. Let's play *Wheel of Fortune!" (The term to be guessed is* peer pressure.*)*

Go to the chalkboard and make lines as shown below.

—— —— —— ——   —— —— —— —— —— —— —— ——

When the students have correctly guessed the words, ask them:

"What is *peer pressure?" (*Peer pressure *has to do with kids who are around your age—your peers—talking you into doing things you don't think you should do.)*

Then say:

"Peer pressure can be broken down into four different categories: obvious negative, subtle negative, obvious positive, and subtle positive."

"The first kind of peer pressure is called *obvious negative.* This is what we think of most often when we think of peer pressure. Imagine that someone asks you to do something you shouldn't, like smoke a cigarette or drink a beer. What you are being asked to do is *obvious*, and it is a behavior that is *negative* or *wrong*. You may experience this kind of peer pressure, but I believe you can say 'No' if you really want to. It is hard, but I have confidence that you can and will say 'No'."

"The second kind of peer pressure is called *subtle negative.* This is the kind of peer pressure that worries me the most, because it is not so obvious. To show you what I mean, let's play a game."

"I want each of you to stand up and move toward the middle of the classroom. I am going to read some alternatives, and each of you is going to have to choose between two things. The kids who prefer one thing will walk to one side of the room, and the kids who like the other thing will go to the opposite side of the classroom. Listen to what I have to say, watch where I am pointing so you will know where to go, and make up your own mind." *(After identifying each of the choices, wait a few seconds for the pressure to develop. During this game, watch very closely. Peer pressure will definitely be at work. Make mental or written notes of what you see. At the end of the game, share with the students what you have observed.)*

Begin the game by saying the following:

> "If you like school, go to that side of the room *(point)*. If you don't like school, go to that side of the room *(point)*."

> "If you would rather have cola, go to that side of the room *(point)*. If you would rather have juice, go to that side of the room *(point)*."

> "If you would rather listen to rock and roll music, go to that side of the room *(point)*. If you would rather listen to country music, go to that side of the room *(point)*."

> "If you like seeing scary movies, go to that side of the room *(point)*. If you don't like seeing scary movies, go to that side of the room *(point)*."

> "If you have stuffed animals on your bed, go to that side of the room *(point)*. If you don't have stuffed animals on your bed, go to that side of the room *(point)*."

Continue this game, using situations that might generate peer pressure, until you feel enough examples have been given for the students to understand the meaning of subtle negative peer pressure. Then say:

"When someone really likes to go to school but sees all of his or her friends going to the side that says they don't like school, that person is under subtle negative peer pressure. It is subtle because no one is actually telling him or her what to do. But because the person wants to be like the rest of the crowd, he or she goes along with the action. It is negative because it isn't what the person really wants to do and because the action is something that doesn't help him or her."

Have the students sit down. Then describe the different examples of subtle negative peer pressure that you observed during the game. (Typical examples: Someone laughing at a choice made by another student, a large group of students standing together and looking smug, a few students standing together looking nervous and trying to explain why they are there.)

Tell the students:

"This is the hardest type of peer pressure to fight, because no one wants to be different. It doesn't matter that, in the game, no one asked anyone to come to a certain side. People were still under subtle negative peer pressure because they saw so many others making a different choice. There will be times when you may be tempted to do things you don't want to do—or that you know you shouldn't do—because you don't want to feel different."

"In the story, it was probably hard for Chris to say to everyone, 'I'm not going to the railroad tracks.' She had to risk losing her friends. In a story, it might sound easy. But in real life, it is difficult to do things that might mean losing friends."

Ask the students the following question:

"Do you think there is such thing as *positive peer pressure*?" *(Yes.)*

Then say:

"*Positive peer pressure* is the opposite of *negative peer pressure.* In positive peer pressure, kids are pressuring other kids to do the right thing. For example: Imagine that a teacher has made a deal with the class that if everyone finished every assignment for a week, the class could have a pizza party. There would probably be a lot of pressure to finish assignments. I imagine that the responsible students would be coaxing the less-dependable students to turn in all their assignments."

Ask the students the following questions:

"Would this situation involve pressure to do something positive or negative?" *(Positive)*

"Do you think this type of pressure is subtle or obvious?" *(Obvious, because someone is encouraging someone else to do something in a very outright manner.)*

Have the students think of other examples of obvious positive peer pressure. Encourage answers that describe situations in which people are talking others into doing the right things, like studying for tests or including everyone in a game.

The last type of peer pressure is *subtle positive.* This type of pressure is subtle because no one actually comes out and asks anyone to do something positive, but a person wants to do the positive thing because everyone else is doing it.

Ask the students the following question:

"What would be some examples of *subtle positive peer pressure?*" *(A group of friends values cleanliness and neatness, so individual members of the group feel pressure to take showers and wear fresh clothes. Or a new kid who has always been aggressive learns to talk out his/her problems because that's what the other kids do.)*

During this discussion, make sure that the students understand and are able to provide examples of all four types of peer pressure.

 Activity: Write each type of peer pressure (1. obvious negative 2. subtle negative 3. obvious positive 4. subtle positive) on a notecard. Divide the class into four groups and have each group draw a card. For larger classes, make two sets of notecards and divide the class into eight groups. Have each group of students role-play to demonstrate a real-life example of the type of peer pressure named on the group's card. Give the students a specified amount of time to prepare their role-play. Then have them enact it for the rest of the class.

 Conclude the lesson by saying:

"There is no magic for fighting peer pressure. But being aware of it may help you. You have to use your brain and make your own decisions. Be aware of the pressures around you. Stand up and do what is right for you!"

LENNY THE BULLY
A Lesson about Breaking the Chain of Violence

MATERIALS NEEDED:

- ✔ Puppet
- ✔ Paper chain
- ✔ Copy of *Break the Chain* (page 121) for each student

LESSON:

The facilitator should:

1 Greet the students and introduce the puppet. Then have the following conversation with the puppet:

> **Facilitator:** "How are you doing today?"
> **Puppet:** "I am upset because this kid at school has been making fun of me."
> **Facilitator:** "Does that kid tease just you or is he that way with everyone?"
> **Puppet:** "He really isn't too nice to anyone. He is a big bully!"
> **Facilitator:** "It seems that there are people who like to push others around. What are you going to do about this problem?"
> **Puppet:** "I don't know what to do."
> **Facilitator:** "Let's talk about it. But first, I want to tell you a story about a bully I once knew."

2 Read or tell the following story:

Lenny is a boy who, sadly, is not very happy with himself or with his life. He doesn't like the way he looks, and he struggles with many of his school subjects. He doesn't feel that he can do anything very well. When Lenny talks to himself, as we all do, he doesn't say very nice things.

Lenny lives alone with his mom. She is a nurse and she often has to work long hours. Since his mom works the early shift, Lenny often wakes up to the sound of a shrill alarm clock. Let me tell you what a typical morning is like for him.

Lenny gets up and stumbles to the bathroom. As he looks in the mirror, he groans, "Look at my hair! It's sticking up again, and nothing I

can do will make it lay down. My nose is getting bigger every day. Why can't *I* grow bigger instead of my stupid nose?"

Then he remembers he has a test in math at school. Math is Lenny's worst subject. He usually flunks his math tests. "Oh, great," he thinks, "I will have another *F*!"

Lenny can't find a clean shirt, so he grabs the one he wore yesterday. It has several spots on the front and it kind of smells bad, but it is all he has. "Nobody better say anything to me about this shirt," he mutters as he walks into the kitchen.

He grabs a piece of toast and heads to the bus stop.

Stop the story at this point and ask the students:

"As Lenny walks to the bus stop, how is he feeling?" *(Rotten!)*

"If Lenny meets someone from his class, how will he greet him or her?" *(If students get stuck, prompt them.)* "Do you think he will smile and say, 'Good morning! You look nice today!'? No, he will probably snarl and say, 'Get out of my way, you jerk!' or push the person out of his way."

"Why would Lenny be mean?" *(Because he feels so bad about himself. Discuss the phrase:* misery loves company*.)*

Continue reading the story:

Well, sure enough, Jack comes along and Lenny says, "What are *you* looking at, moron?"

Stop the story at this point and ask the students:

"How does this make Jack feel?" *(Rotten!)*

"If someone comes to the bus stop right now, how will Jack greet him or her?" *(He will probably be rude, too.)*

Continue reading the story:

Sure enough, Sandra comes along and Jack laughs and says, "Where did you get that outfit, in the garbage dump?" Jack and Lenny laugh loudly.

Stop the story at this point and ask the students:

"How does this make Sandra feel?" *(Rotten!)*

Lively Lessons

"How might she be tempted to treat others?" *(In the same manner)*

At this point, discuss with the students how what is happening right now in the story is like a chain. Show the students a portion of a paper chain. Hold it up and say:

"On a chain, one link is dependent on the next. What is the only thing that will stop the chain from continuing? The chain must be broken!" *(Dramatically rip the chain apart.)*

Point out that this chain is made of paper, but that even the strongest chain can be broken.

Ask the students:

"How can the 'chain' in the story be broken?" *(Someone should ignore the insults or try to be kind to Lenny and the others.)*

Through discussion, try to get the students to see that Lenny is a victim, too. He has had many failures and when he compares himself to others, he finds himself lacking. Knowing how Lenny feels about himself may help students understand why he is so mean and even sympathize with him. Suggest that although there are other bullies who are like Lenny, not all bullies are bullies for the same reasons. Some may feel superior or enjoy having the power to make others feel bad. Some people may be bullies because they don't stop to think about the feelings of others.

With this in mind, have the students brainstorm about how the chain of bullying could be broken. What could they do if they were to encounter a bully?

Ideas should include:

- Ignore him/her. *(Victims should mentally remind themselves of their good qualities and not believe what the bully is saying.)*

- Discuss the problem with an adult.

  (The following ideas must be used with caution. Warn students that some bullies can be dangerous and should not be provoked!)

- Give the bully an "I Message." *(I feel _____ because you _____ and I would like you to _____ .)* "I Messages" must be delivered assertively. Whining or bullying back do not help.

- Try being kind to the bully even though he/she is not kind to anyone. If the bully is included in an invitation to play a game, he/she may feel better about him/herself. *(Timing is important here. You wouldn't respond to an insult by inviting someone to play. But at a later date, you might try it.)*

• Humor can sometimes be effective, but use caution. If the bully thinks you are laughing at him/her, he/she could get angry! An example of humor diffusing a situation: Lenny says, "Your hair looks like it got cut by hedge clippers." The other child smiles and says, "I told that barber to use scissors instead of those trimmers!" *(Note: Humor should NOT be directed AT bullies! They usually can't take a joke!)*

3. Suggest to the students that if the bullying-behavior chain could be broken, maybe a new kind of chain could be started. Is it possible that a friendly chain could be started? Ask students what a friendly chain would be like.

4. Conclude the lesson by distributing a copy of *Break the Chain* and a pencil to each student. Have the students start with Lenny and show how they might break the chain and what could happen if they did. On the left side of the chain, write statements that Lenny might make. *(Caution students not to go overboard and not to use profanity.)* In the broken section, write what the person did to break the chain. On the right side of the chain, write some comments that could be the start of a positive chain.

BREAK THE CHAIN

_____

_____

_____

_____

_____

_____

_____

_____

_____

_____

_____

_____

_____

_____

WAR AND PEACE
A Lesson about Conflict-Resolution

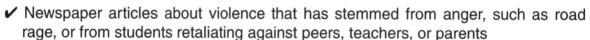

Note: This lesson is best conducted in two sessions.

SESSION 1:

MATERIALS NEEDED:

✔ Puppet
✔ *Conflict-Resolution Steps Chart* made on posterboard with the following four steps:

1. Calm down.
2. Talk, listen, and identify the problem.
3. Brainstorm solutions.
4. Agree on a solution that everyone accepts.

✔ Newspaper articles about violence that has stemmed from anger, such as road rage, or from students retaliating against peers, teachers, or parents
✔ Copy of the *Conflict-Resolution Song* (page 131) for each student

LESSON:

The facilitator should:

 Greet the students and introduce the puppet. Then have the following conversation with the puppet:

Facilitator:	"Hi, (<u>NAME OF PUPPET</u>)! How are you feeling today?"
Puppet:	"I am so mad!"
Facilitator:	"What's the matter? Why are you mad?"
Puppet:	"My brother took too long a turn on the computer and now I am grounded."
Facilitator:	"That doesn't sound right. Tell me what happened."
Puppet:	"Well, I got mad at him and then we got into a big fight. I punched him, and now I am grounded. But it's really not fair because it was all his fault."
Facilitator:	"I guess your mom was hoping that you could settle the problem without fighting."
Puppet:	"She is pretty sick of our fighting. I just get so mad because he is so selfish."
Facilitator:	"It sounds like you need help. I think today's lesson might be just the answer you need."

Lively Lessons

Ask the students:

"How many of you ever get mad at your brothers or sisters or friends and end up in trouble like (<u>NAME OF PUPPET</u>)?" *(No answer is required. Students can just raise their hands.)*

Then say:

"You know, conflicts are part of life. Whenever two people are together for a while, there are bound to be disagreements. But a disagreement doesn't have to end in a fight. Let me tell you a story about two sisters who had to learn this lesson for themselves."

 Read or tell the following story:

Once upon a time, there were two sisters named Kathy and Debra. Kathy was 10 years old and Debra was 11. They lived with their dad in a tiny two-bedroom apartment.

Ever since they could remember, the girls have shared a bedroom. And ever since they could remember, they have fought about sharing a room.

"Kathy, your sweater is on my bed! If I see it there again, I'm putting it in the trash!" screamed Debra.

"Well, your smelly socks are on *my* side of the room!" yelled Kathy.

"Those aren't my socks, and your side of the room looks like a pig sty! I am sick of your mess!" Debra screamed back.

The fights went on and on. Sometimes the sisters got so mad at each other they would actually start punching, kicking, pinching, and biting each other. When that happened, their dad would usually have to run into their room, pull them apart, and act as a referee. Sometimes he would tell the girls that they were grounded and had to stay in their room, which only meant more togetherness and more fights.

One night, there was a fight that really got out of control. Kathy wanted to turn the radio on and Debra wanted the room quiet so she could read. They started arguing and called each other some terrible names that I won't even mention here. They both got so mad that they started swinging at each other and Kathy's fist connected with Debra's eye. Their dad came into the room when he heard Debra screaming. Her eye was already beginning to puff up and turn a horrible shade of purple.

He got some ice for Debra's eye and then he sat down on one of the beds. He looked very discouraged, very tired, and very serious. He said, "Girls, we can't go on living this way. There is no peace in this house at all. It is like we are living in a war zone! I really don't know how to stop you from fighting, but I cannot tolerate it anymore. Somebody is going to get seriously hurt. Right now, I am thinking that I will have to send one of you away to live with your grandmom. I don't want to split you apart, but I guess there is no other answer. I am going to take a week to think this over. Then I guess I will have to decide which one of you will go."

With that, Dad got up and left the room. Debra and Kathy stared at each other. As much as they fought, they did not like the idea of living apart from each other. "What are we going to do?" asked Kathy.

Debra said, "Well, we'd better think of an answer. Or in one week, one of us will be packing."

Kathy suggested that they each get out a piece of paper and write down the reasons why they fought so much. She said, "I will go to the kitchen and write, and you stay here."

So Kathy took her piece of paper to the kitchen table and thought about their fights. She thought about the fact that some of the fights started about little things like socks and then got bigger and bigger. Both of the girls had bad tempers and seemed to turn little issues into big problems. Sometimes, she thought, their fights started because the room seemed too little for both of them, and Debra did not seem to respect her space.

Kathy began to write. In the other room, Debra was making a similar list.

When the sisters got back together, Debra asked Kathy what she had written. Kathy said, "Number 1 is that we have to share such a small room. Number 2 is that neither of us tries to control our temper. Number 3 is that you are neat and I am messy. What did you write?"

Debra said, "Number 1 is that we lose our tempers. Number 2 is that we don't think about each other's feelings, and Number 3 is that you are messy and I am neat."

The girls looked at each other and began laughing. "I know that if we stay calm, we can work out a plan," said Kathy. "It looks to me like we both have to start with our tempers."

Debra said that the school counselor had just presented a lesson on anger and how to manage it. She got her notes out and shared them with her sister. One of the suggestions in her notes was that if either person started to lose control, he or she would signal the other person. It was sort of like a warning signal. This sounded like a good idea to both Kathy and Debra. They agreed to work on controlling their tempers by signalling one another if either one started losing control.

"Now," said Kathy, "since we are both calm and thinking, let's work out a plan for how we can live in such a tiny space in peace."

They talked for almost an hour. Each girl told the other what was important to her, what space she absolutely needed, and what she could live without. They planned carefully and wrote out a schedule for the week that gave each of them the room space she felt she needed at specific times.

When Kathy and Debra finished talking with each other, they went to talk with their dad. They asked him to wait a month before he called their grandmom so they could prove that they could live in peace. Dad was relieved. Ever since the girls' mother had died, he had tried to keep the family together. Grandmom was always willing to help, but he really didn't want to send either of his daughters away.

It has now been six months since the night of the black eye. There have been disagreements, but there hasn't been one fight. Kathy and Debra have learned to resolve their conflicts peaceably, and their family has been living happily ever after!

 Discuss the story by asking the following questions:

"What were the reasons that Kathy and Debra fought?" *(They had to share a small room and had different ideas about how the room should look. When disagreements occurred, they didn't try to control their tempers.)*

"Their fights started with little disagreements. How did the little disagreements get bigger?" *(They kept yelling back and forth at each other. The more they yelled, the angrier they got. Finally, they lost control of their tempers and started fighting. The girls didn't realize that maybe there was a way to work out their problems if they stayed calm. Anger blinded them to possible solutions for plans of sharing a small room.)*

"What made them finally try to settle their problems without fighting?" *(The possibility of having to move apart from each other gave them a reason to want to solve their arguments peaceably, and that is always the first step. You have to want to work things out.)*

"Animals frequently fight with each other, using claws and teeth. People don't need to resort to this type of fighting because we have the use of something that animals don't have. What is that?" *(Ability to think and to use words and logic)*

Then say:

"Some people resort to violence because they don't know how to settle things any other way. Violence is a real problem in our society today. TV and movies make it seem glamorous to fight. But in the movies, the stars get up, take their paychecks, and go home. In real life, people are hurt, killed, or end up in prison for doing the things we see actors do on TV and in the movies." *(Display the newspaper articles pertaining to children and violence to illustrate this point.)*

 Tell the students that today's lesson will be the first of two lessons in which the class members will be talking about how to settle their differences peaceably. The correct title for this type of lesson is *Conflict-Resolution.*

Ask the students:

"What do you think the word *conflict* means?" *(Conflict is a word used to describe a situation in which two people or sides disagree about something. Disagreements, arguments, fights, and even wars fall into this category.)*

Then say:

"It is not necessary for conflicts to erupt into fights and wars. All conflicts can be resolved peaceably if people who are angry with each other follow the basic steps of conflict-resolution." *(Show the* Conflict-Resolution Steps Chart *and review the four steps with the students.)*

"In order to be able to understand and use these steps, you must first learn how to control and manage your anger, which is what we will discuss next."

ANGER

Tell the students:

"Anger is a very powerful emotion that all people experience. When a person becomes angry, it is often a signal that there is a problem that needs to be solved. But many people become so overwhelmed with being angry that they can't deal effectively with the problem. You might hear people say, 'I can't help it, I have a bad temper.' But that is not true. People can learn to control their tempers, if they want to. The younger you are when you learn to control your anger, the better it is. This is because if you wait until you are older, your anger becomes more powerful. And the more powerful it is, the harder it is to control. That is why we are going to learn about anger now and learn to identify the situations that trigger our anger. It is important to recognize:

1. the situations that make you angry.

   (Have the students name situations that make them angry. Summarize and rephrase each situation as it is named. For example:

Michael:	*"I get angry when I don't get a turn to bat at recess."*
Facilitator:	*"So when things seem unfair, you get angry."*

After a while, the students will note common themes, such as unfairness, protecting themselves from attacks, teasing, etc. If there is time, explain that it is not the situation *that makes a person angry, but the way he/she* views *the situation and the kinds of things the person says to him/herself when the situation occurs. For example, when Michael didn't get a turn to bat at recess, he got angry because he was thinking, "The kids are being mean to me. They put me last in line on purpose! I hate them!" He viewed the situation as being unfair, not looking at the fact that the recess ended before he got a turn at bat. He told himself things that made him even more angry.)*

2. what happens to your body when you are angry.

   Let's say that something happens that you think is unfair. You begin to feel angry. You may feel different sensations in your body. Something called *adrenaline* begins pumping through your body. All of a sudden, you have a lot of energy. You may have felt tired before, but now you aren't tired. You are mad, and your anger is similar to a volcanic eruption. It starts small and builds to an explosive level. It is important that you be able to tell when you are becoming angry, and that you recognize what your body is telling you. It will help you catch the anger before you lose control.

3. that you are feeling angry and it is time to do some things to calm yourself down. Some ways to calm down are:

   - Count to 10.
   - Breath deeply (at least three times).
   - Talk to yourself and say calming things.
   - Move, walk, expend the energy that comes with anger." *(This does not mean punching something. Punching a pillow may seem harmless, but it seems to indicate that you need to use your fist.)*

Ask the students:

   "Can you think of any other ways to calm down?" *(Some may say they go to their rooms. Encourage the students to think of strategies that they can use regardless of where they are.)*

 Activity: Tell the students that they are going to role-play calming down. Select a volunteer. Tell the volunteer that his/her brother just grabbed the last soda in the refrigerator. The volunteer feels angry, because the brother just drank a soda that was his/hers. Have the student role-play a method that could be used to calm him/herself down. Then select another volunteer to role-play the same situation. This time, tell the volunteer to use a method that is different from the one already presented. Continue the role-plays until all the students have given examples of several methods.

Mar✳co Products, Inc.

Bring out the puppet. Ask the puppet if he/she is beginning to understand what he/she could have done to solve the problem with his/her brother. Tell the puppet and the students:

> "Calming down is only the first step. Now you need to learn how to resolve the conflict. This is what we will discuss the next time we meet."

7 Conclude the session by distributing a copy of the *Conflict-Resolution Song* to each student and teaching them to sing it to the tune of *Pop, Goes the Weasel!*

SESSION 2

MATERIALS NEEDED:

- ✔ Puppet
- ✔ *Conflict-Resolution Steps Chart* from Session 1
- ✔ Chalkboard and chalk
- ✔ Copy of *Conflict-Resolution* (pages 132-133) and a pencil for each student group

LESSON:

The facilitator should:

 Greet the students. Using the puppet, have the following conversation:

Facilitator:	"How is it going with your brother?"
Puppet:	"Well, I have really been working on calming myself down, but he is still hogging the computer."
Facilitator:	"Then it's a good thing that today we are going to learn the rest of the steps to conflict-resolution. Using these ideas with what you already know will help you solve your problem."

 Show the *Conflict-Resolution Steps Chart* and review the following four steps:

1. Calm down.
2. Talk, listen, and identify the problem.
3. Brainstorm solutions.
4. Agree on a solution that everyone accepts.

Say to the students:

> "We spent the last lesson talking about Step #1. *(Point to Step #1 on the chart.)* Who remembers some ways that will help you calm down?" *(Count to 10. Breathe deeply at least three times. Talk to yourself and say calming things. Move to get rid of the energy that comes with anger.)*

Then say:

"Some people think that when you get angry, you calm down and forget the whole thing. Wrong! There was a problem to begin with and the problem still exists. That leads us to Step #2. *(Point to Step #2 on the chart.)* Step #2 says that the people involved with the problem need to talk, listen, and identify the problem."

"Let's go back to the story about Kathy and Debra. Once they calmed down, they had to identify the problem, which was that they had to share a small room and had different opinions about how it needed to be kept. To reach this point, they had to share their ideas and feelings. Each one needed to be able to talk, and each one had to listen to the other. Using "I Messages" is an excellent way to communicate needs. These are sentences that begin with the word *I* instead of with the word *You.* It's important to remember that when you are identifying the problem, you must not blame anyone for causing it."

"Our puppet friend keeps saying that his brother hogs the computer. That is his opinion. The real problem is that there is one computer that both brothers want to use. Saying it that way makes it clear to everyone what the situation is that needs a solution."

"Once we have identified the problem, we can go on to Step #3. *(Point to Step #3 on the chart.)* This is *brainstorming solutions.* Because there are probably lots of ways to settle any problem, the people involved should make a list of possible solutions. *Getting everyone's ideas about a problem* is what *brainstorming* means. Don't stop at one or two ideas. To help you think of solutions, use the headings: Win/Win, Win/Lose, Lose/Win, or Lose/Lose. *(Write the headings on the chalkboard.)* For example: Cindy and Judi are doing a science project together. Cindy wants to do the project on animals. Judi wants to do the project on plants. When they brainstormed solutions to the problem, they came up with the following:

Win/Lose:

- They toss a coin and Cindy wins.
- Judi gives in because Cindy has lots of information they could use on the project.

The Lose/Win solutions are the opposite of the Win/Lose solutions. Judi wins and Cindy loses.

Lose/Win:

- They toss a coin and Judi wins.
- Cindy gives in because Judi has information they could use on the project.

Win/Win

- They do the report on plant-eating animals. (They both win!)

- One girl could get her way this time and the next time they do a project, the other girl gets to pick the subject.

Lose/Lose

- They decide not to work together because they cannot agree.
- One person does a poor job and their overall grade is lower.
- They pick a totally different subject that they both like and that they can agree on." *(Neither girl gets her original choice. Sometimes to settle an argument neither person can get his/her own way, and this can be a positive solution.)*

"If you use these categories when thinking of solutions, you will generate ideas that might otherwise have been overlooked."

"The last Step is #4. *(Point to Step #4 on the chart.)* It is to choose a solution that they can agree on."

 Divide the students into groups. Distribute a copy of *Conflict-Resolution* and a pencil to each group. Tell each group to elect a leader who will write down the answers that the group decides upon. Explain that the leader will read each situation. Then the group members are to identify the problem and brainstorm solutions, using the Win/Win, Win/Lose, Lose/Win, and Lose/Lose headings. When the group decides upon an answer, the leader should circle the appropriate decision. When the worksheets are completed, have each group share its solutions with the class.

 Take out the puppet and have the following conversation:

Facilitator:	"Do you have any thoughts about how you will work out the problems with your brother?"
Puppet:	"I have some ideas that will be Win/Win for us, but we will have to sit down and talk it out together. I hope he will agree."
Facilitator:	"Well, if you both stay calm, I believe you will be able to solve the problem. Good luck!"

 Conclude the lesson by teaching the students to sing the following rap.

We can learn to work and play,
In peace without one fight.
If we try to get along,
Then everything's all right!

With effort we can compromise,
Or sometimes try to vote.
Win/Win, Win/Lose, if we cooperate,
No one ever needs to gloat.

CONFLICT–RESOLUTION SONG
(Sung to the tune of *Pop, Goes the Weasel!*)

When you get angry during the day,

And you don't think you can stand it,

Don't store the anger, calm yourself down.

Don't pop! Breathe! Discuss it.

If you have trouble controlling yourself,

And you seem to be losing your temper,

Always remember to calm yourself down.

Don't pop! Breathe! Discuss it.

Exercise, just moving around,

Helps to make you feel good.

Just make sure you work it out.

Don't pop! Breathe! Discuss it.

CONFLICT RESOLUTION

1. There are two fifth-grade classrooms. They are planning a field trip together. (The bus costs too much for one class alone.) The students in Mrs. Sterling's class have voted and agreed that they want to go to the Science Center. Mr. Miller's class wants to go to the Wildlife Park. All the kids have been fighting about it at recess. How can this be settled?

    Win/Lose _____

    Lose/Win _____

    Win/Win _____

    Lose/Lose _____

2. At a lunchtime kickball game, John tagged Lucy out, but Lucy said that John missed her. The teammates agreed with their own players and a big fight broke out. What could they have done to settle the fight? What could be done so that this won't happen again?

    Win/Lose _____

    Lose/Win _____

    Win/Win _____

    Lose/Lose _____

3. Adam accidentally tripped Todd. Todd, who has a very quick temper, didn't think it was an accident. He pushed Adam down and started swinging. What could Adam have done?

    Win/Lose _____

    Lose/Win _____

    Win/Win _____

    Lose/Lose _____

4. Jeffrey and Michael are good athletes. Both of them like to win and they seem to have problems at every recess. If they are on the same team, their team always wins. If they are on opposite teams, one will do something that will anger the other (such as bragging about winning), and there is always a fight. What can be done?

    Win/Lose _____

    Lose/Win _____

    Win/Win _____

    Lose/Lose _____

Lively Lessons

5. Mr. Thompson's class has an assignment. Everyone is to do a report on one of the 50 states and then share the report with the rest of the class. Everyone is supposed to pick a different state. Molly was born in Texas, so she wants to do her report on Texas. Ellen wants Texas, too, because she lived there for a while. The girls keep arguing, and Mr. Thompson has said they have to work it out themselves. How can they settle this?

Win/Lose _____

Lose/Win _____

Win/Win _____

Lose/Lose _____

6. Jamie brought a new calculator to school. While she was showing Trent the calculator, he dropped it and it broke. Jamie got really mad and said that Trent owed her a new calculator. Trent said it was an accident and that he didn't owe her anything. An argument broke out, and the teacher came over to see what had happened. How could this be settled?

Win/Lose _____

Lose/Win _____

Win/Win _____

Lose/Lose _____

7. Sherri, Julie, and Janet are all good friends. Sherri's birthday is coming up, and Julie and Janet want to give her a party. They can't agree on anything! Julie wants it to be a surprise party and Janet doesn't. Janet wants to have the party at her house, but Julie wants it to be at a place like the skating rink or a restaurant. They are arguing about every idea either of them has. What can they do?

Win/Lose _____

Lose/Win _____

Win/Win _____

Lose/Lose _____

ROGER THE VET
A Lesson on Career Awareness

MATERIALS NEEDED:

✔ Copy of *Career Pathways* (page 138), copy of *Career Graph* (page 139), and a pencil for each student

LESSON:

The facilitator should:

Greet the students and say:

> "We are going to be spending some time exploring the world of work and learning about careers. We're doing this because it is important that you be aware of all the possibilities ahead of you. How many of you think you already know what you are going to be when you grow up? *(Usually, many respond* Yes.*)* This could be a problem. Let me tell you a story about a boy who made up his mind, too!"

Read or tell the following story:

> **From the time Roger was old enough to walk, talk, and understand the world around him, he knew that he loved animals. His family had a dog and a cat, and Roger was always with his pets. They slept on his bed at night and he thought of them as family. Roger loved to take care of his pets. He was always brushing them, feeding them, walking them, and tending to their needs.**
>
> **Roger's dog and cat were not the only animals he cared for. He was constantly bringing home stray rabbits, birds with hurt wings, or turtles that he had found on the road. All of Roger's friends joked that he could open his own zoo.**
>
> **When Roger was old enough to understand that when you grow up, you could actually get paid to take care of animals, he made up his mind. That's what he was going to do: He was going to be a veterinarian.**
>
> **When Roger was in elementary school, lessons about jobs were taught every year. These lessons were called career–awareness programs. They began with community helpers who visited the kindergarten**

class. Each year, there were lessons about all the different kinds of jobs boys and girls might want to do when they got older. Roger usually listened with only one ear, because he already knew he was going to be a veterinarian. He didn't need to know about different careers or about what he was interested in or anything else to do with the career lessons. Maybe these lessons could be helpful to someone else, but not to him.

Actually, Roger didn't pay much attention to any of the subjects at school. He didn't even *like* school, because it kept him away from his animals. His mind was always on what his pets might be doing or wondering whether any of them needed him. He couldn't wait to get home every day to tend to their needs. There were many nights when his homework did not get completed because, in his opinion, he had more important things to do.

When Roger was in middle school, there were more lessons on careers. They even had a Career Day one year. But again, Roger tuned the whole thing out. Why? Because he already knew what he was going to be. He was going to be a _____. *(Let the students say in unison: "Veterinarian.")*

In high school, there was even more talk about making a career choice. When the school had a Job Fair, Roger didn't bother to attend because he knew what he was going to be. He was going to be a _____. *(Let the students say in unison: "Veterinarian.")* He didn't keep appointments with the school counselor, either. He saw no reason to visit the counselor when he didn't need help. He was going to be a _____. *(Let the students say in unison: "Veterinarian.")*

One day when Roger was a senior in high school, his dog became very sick. Until this illness, Roger had always tended to his dog's simple needs and his mother had always taken his pets to the veterinarian for their shots and check-ups. He had never had to take his dog to the vet before. But this time, Roger's mother was busy and she asked him to do it.

As Dr. Martin, the veterinarian, examined his dog, Roger talked. He said, "You know, I am a senior and I have decided that I am going to be a veterinarian, too."

Dr. Martin said, "Great! What college are you going to be attending?"

Roger was stunned, "College? I'm not planning to go to college. I already know a lot about animals, and I plan to open an animal clinic next year."

"Son, don't you know that you just can't call yourself a veterinarian? It takes years of schooling. You need to get an undergraduate degree, then you must get accepted at and attend veterinary school," explained Dr. Martin.

Roger replied, "But I don't even *like* going to school!"

"Well," said Dr. Martin, "to be a vet, you have to keep going to school for years. I hope you like science, because you will have to take lots of science courses while you are in school."

Roger said, "But I *hate* science!"

By this time in the conversation, the vet was giving Roger's dog a shot. The dog yelped.

Roger said, "Hey, you hurt my dog!"

Dr. Martin said, "Sometimes you have to hurt animals in order to cure them. And I'm afraid that sometimes, no matter what you do, you can't save an animal. I have had to put many animals to sleep."

Roger said, "I could never do that!"

"Son, I am afraid that being a vet may not be for you. I think you need to think this over," Dr. Martin advised.

Roger went home that day totally confused. He had never in his life considered anything else besides being a veterinarian. He really did not know what to do.

Well, I'm afraid that the story does not have a happy ending. Roger is now 26 years old. He has a job at a veterinarian's office, but he doesn't get to work much with the animals. He helps by cleaning the office and the cages.

 Discuss the story by asking the following questions:

"What was Roger's problem?" *(He closed his mind early in his life and chose a career that really wasn't the best choice for him.)*

"What didn't Roger find out about being a veterinarian that could have been helpful to him?" *(Roger didn't know how long he had to attend school, what kinds of courses he would have to take, what the unpleasant aspects of the job are.)*

4 Then say:

> "At this time in your life, you don't have to know what you want to do when you are an adult. Nobody expects you to decide that yet. At this time in your life, you are expected to learn about different careers and the options that might be open to you."

Ask the following question:

> "How do you think a person finds the job that is right for him or her?" *(If these answers are not given, write them on the chalkboard:*
>
> 1. *People learn about themselves by knowing their strengths, weaknesses, interests, and values.*
> 2. *People learn about many different jobs. There are hundreds of thousands of different careers. The perfect career for a person may be something that he or she has never even heard of or a career that hasn't been invented yet! People have to learn and explore and start thinking about the type of job in which they may be interested.*
> 3. *People begin to match themselves to certain types of work.)*

5 **Activity:** Distribute a copy of *Career Pathways*, a copy of *Career Graph,* and a pencil to each student. Have the students read the information written on the *Career Pathways* sheet and rate each area from 1 to 10 according to their interests and strengths. Emphasize that this is a *subjective* interest sheet. They estimate and fill in a number that seems right to them. When the students have finished, have them transfer their numbers to the squares opposite the topic on the *Career Graph* sheet. Then they should make a bar graph to show their results. Discuss the results of the bar graph, whether the students feel it is accurate for them, and whether they were surprised by the results.

6 Conclude the lesson by encouraging the students to use different sources to investigate jobs along the path indicated on the bar graph. If desired, assign interviews, reports, etc.

CAREER PATHWAYS

Which path do you want to take in the future? Everyone is different. We all have different strengths and weaknesses and we are all interested in different things. In planning for your future career, you need to first think about yourself and then investigate various career clusters to find which pathway might be right for you.

Consider the following questions about six career clusters. Rate yourself from 1 to 10, using 1 to indicate low interest and strengths and 10 to indicate high interest and strengths.

1. **ARTS AND COMMUNICATIONS:** Are you a creative thinker? Do you like to use your imagination, enjoy thinking up new ideas, and like to share your thoughts and ideas with others? If so, this could be the career path for you!

    1   2   3   4   5   6   7   8   9   10

2. **BUSINESS, MANAGEMENT, AND TECHNOLOGY:** Do you like being a leader, organizing people, planning activities for others, and talking with important people? *or* Do you like working with numbers or ideas, like to carry through an idea and see the end product, like to know what is expected of you, and like things around you to be neat and orderly? If so, this could be the career path for you!

    1   2   3   4   5   6   7   8   9   10

3. **HEALTH SERVICES:** Do you like helping people who are sick or helping people stay well? Are you interested in new diseases and in how the body works? Do you like observing people and looking for changes in their physical well-being? If so, this could be the career path for you!

    1   2   3   4   5   6   7   8   9   10

4. **HUMAN SERVICES:** Are you friendly, open, outgoing, understanding, and cooperative? Do you like to work with people to help solve problems? Is it important to you to do something that makes things better for other people? If so, this could be the career path for you!

    1   2   3   4   5   6   7   8   9   10

5. **INDUSTRIAL AND ENGINEERING TECHNOLOGY:** Are you mechanically inclined and practical? Do you like to use your hands and build things? Do you like to know how things work? If so, this could be the career path for you!

    1   2   3   4   5   6   7   8   9   10

6. **NATURAL RESOURCES:** Are you a nature lover, curious about the physical world, interested in plants and animals? Do you like to be physically active, observe, learn, investigate, or solve problems? If so, this could be the career path for you!

    1   2   3   4   5   6   7   8   9   10

CAREER GRAPH

COMPUTER CRATER

SEA OF SCIENCE

FUTURE CAREER CHOICES

MOUNT MEDICAL

CAREER EDUCATION

A.   Arts and Communications

B.   Business, Management, and Technology

C.   Health Services

D.   Human Services

E.   Industrial and Engineering Technology

F.   Natural Resources

	A	B	C	D	E	F
10						
9						
8						
7						
6						
5						
4						
3						
2						
1						

DRUGS AND ALCOHOL INFORMATION GAME
A Lesson on Substance–Abuse for Grades 4–5

MATERIALS NEEDED:

✔ A tagboard "Yes" sign and a tagboard "No" sign for each team (Make the "Yes" signs a different color than the "No" signs.)
✔ Copy of *Score Sheet* (page 144) and a pencil for each team
✔ Small prize for each student (optional)

LESSON:

The facilitator should:

 Greet the students and introduce the lesson by telling them:

> "Today we are going to discuss drugs and alcohol. Some of the things we talk about you may already know. Others may be new. In either case, the information you hear today can help you make appropriate decisions about drugs and alcohol. Since you have had lessons like this before, you probably know quite a bit about drugs and alcohol. So instead of telling you the information, I'm going to let you tell me what you know."

 Divide the students into teams of about three to five members. Distribute a set of signs, a score sheet, and a pencil to each team. Then say:

> "I am going to ask you some questions about drugs and alcohol. Each question can be answered with either "Yes" or "No." As a team, you must discuss whether to raise the "Yes" sign or the "No" sign. Choose someone in your group to raise your answer sign when the (<u>TELL WHAT SIGNAL YOU WILL GIVE</u>) is given. Choose another member of your team to be the scorekeeper. The team will score five points for each correct answer, but no points for each incorrect answer."

 Read the following statements aloud to the students. After each team has selected its answer, read the correct answer and have each team record its points.

1. Some children as young as nine and 10 have drug problems. (***True**—This is why we are having this lesson!*)

2. The drug in cigarette tobacco is called caffeine. (***False**—It is nicotine.*)

3. One drop of pure nicotine is fatal to humans. (***True**—It is poison. *)

4. Research has shown that smokers often get more wrinkles around the eyes than non-smokers do. (*True—Smoking also deadens taste buds and the sense of smell.*)

5. Smoking marijuana harms a person's lungs as much as smoking tobacco does. (*False—It's worse. One marijuana cigarette can do as much damage as 20 tobacco cigarettes.*)

6. When people stop smoking, they can reverse some of the damage that has been done. (*True—Unless the damage has already had permanent consequences.*)

7. Alcohol is a depressant drug that slows body processes. (*True—Some drugs speed things up, but alcohol slows everything down.*)

8. Cancer is the leading cause of death among 15- to 24-year-olds. (*False—Drinking and driving-related accidents are the greatest single cause of death in this age group.*)

9. A one-ounce shot of whiskey has more alcohol than a 12-ounce beer. (*False—They have the same amount.*)

10. Coffee, cold showers, or exercise will help a person sober up. (*False—Only time will sober a person up because the liver has to have time to filter the alcohol out of the bloodstream.*)

11. *Tolerance* means you need more of a drug to get the same effect. (*True—Cigarette smokers gradually find they must smoke more to get the same effect. The same is true with alcohol or other drugs.*)

12. Smoking cigarettes can lead to smoking marijuana. (*True—More than 80% of teens who smoke cigarettes go on to try marijuana. Only 21% of non-smokers try marijuana. Cigarettes are gateway drugs.*)

13. Everyone who drinks becomes an alcoholic. (*False—One out of 10 drinkers becomes an alcoholic.*)

14. If one of your parents is an alcoholic, you are more likely to become an alcoholic. (*True—Research shows that alcoholism has both a genetic and a social link.*)

15. A person can become addicted to crack after using it only once. (*True—That's all it takes.*)

16. Marijuana chemicals leave the body quickly. (*False—The chemicals in marijuana can remain in the body 4-6 weeks.*)

17. *Inhalants* are chemicals found in household products such as cleaners, paints, glues, and solvents. When breathed in, inhalants can cause confusion, loss of self-control, violent behavior, unconsciousness, or death. (**True**—*But kids don't always believe it.*)

18. Smoking marijuana slows down a person's heartbeat. (**False**—*It speeds it up.*)

19. Being an alcoholic means that the person drinks every day. (**False**—*An alcoholic is a person who cannot tolerate any amount of alcohol. Some alcoholics drink only on weekends.*)

20. If you feel sad, it is okay to eat an extra piece of cake. (**False**—*You shouldn't use food or any substance to make you feel better or happy.*)

21. You can become addicted to medicine prescribed by the doctor. (**True**—*Many drugs can be addictive. That is why you should take medicines only as directed by your doctor.*)

22. Caffeine—which can be found in coffee, tea, chocolate, and soda—is a drug. (**True**—*A drug is a substance that changes the way your mind or body works.*)

23. More people are addicted to crack than to any other drug. (**False**—*More people are addicted to alcohol than to any other drug.*)

24. Smoking cigarettes can lead to automobile accidents. (**True**—*Smoking 10 cigarettes in closed car can produce enough carbon monoxide to interfere with a driver's ability to judge time. That could lead to not applying the brakes in time or cutting off another car because the driver thought he/she had time to move into its lane.*)

25. The mind-altering drug in marijuana is called THC. (**True**—*It makes the heart beat faster, but slows down a person's ability to think and move.*)

26. LSD and Angel Dust are hallucinogens and can cause confusion and fear. (**True**—*They can also bring on "bad trips" and "flashbacks."*)

27. The cigarette smokers who are most likely to develop lung cancer as adults are those who begin smoking after the age of 15. (**False**—*It's those who begin before the age of 15.*)

28. After cocaine or crack wears off, the user feels sad and depressed. (**True**—*And then he or she wants more!*)

29. Smoking is known to kill more people than any other drug. (**True**—*Smoking is known as slow-motion suicide. Smoking kills more than 350,000 people a year.*)

Conclude the lesson by having each team total its points. Do not have the teams announce their scores, but say that all of them are winners if they learned even one new fact. If desired, a small token prize can be given to each student.

SOURCES:

Lawless, Scott & Beth Schecter. *Just Say No Club Book*. Just Say No International. Produced by Healy-Wels Communications and James Stockton & Associates, 1987.

Gerne, Timothy A. Jr. & Patricia Gerne. *Substance Abuse Activities For Elementary Children*. Englewood Cliffs, NJ: Prentice Hall, 1986.

Skills For Growing (1990) Canada: Quest International, National PTA, National Association of Elementary School Principals, Lions Clubs International, 1990.

SCORE SHEET

TEAM NAME

Score 5 points for each correct answer.
Score 0 for each incorrect answer.

1. _____
2. _____
3. _____
4. _____
5. _____
6. _____
7. _____
8. _____
9. _____
10. _____
11. _____
12. _____
13. _____
14. _____
15. _____
16. _____
17. _____
18. _____
19. _____
20. _____
21. _____
22. _____
23. _____
24. _____
25. _____
26. _____
27. _____
28. _____
29. _____

TOTAL SCORE _____

SCORE SHEET

TEAM NAME

Score 5 points for each correct answer.
Score 0 for each incorrect answer.

1. _____
2. _____
3. _____
4. _____
5. _____
6. _____
7. _____
8. _____
9. _____
10. _____
11. _____
12. _____
13. _____
14. _____
15. _____
16. _____
17. _____
18. _____
19. _____
20. _____
21. _____
22. _____
23. _____
24. _____
25. _____
26. _____
27. _____
28. _____
29. _____

TOTAL SCORE _____